Thoughts and Reflections Vol 2

By David R B Nicoll

Poetry index:

D0278796

*= Photograph or poem with matching photograph,

All photos by David unless otherwise stated.

Bay

Be you

Being sown

Chugga chug*

Compare*

Designs*

Doubt*

Bad taste

Breakfast

Treat it so! CD cover*

The But n Ben*

Thoughts and Reflections Vol 1 cover photo by Michael de Saedeleer

Of canal surface in Manchester, England. RIP Mike my friend.

Cheaper

Big chief*

Cocktails

Boo*

His neck

By*

Booze

Brother

Captivity

CDs

Coin

Daddy

Do you

Fire*

Drunken driving*

Charlene*

Poetic license

Day

Desire

Die

Do me

Earnings

Escape

Face

Few

Feeds you

For free

For sure

Forty nine

Frustrated

Fun*

Evil*

Everyone*

Energy and light*

Head*

Hear and see*

Hi Steve

Hold my hand

Honestly

I am too

It up

I mean

In tears

Into the future

It go

It

Anything*

African thyme*

Awesome*

Hakuna matata sign on the But N Ben treehouse in Niaberi overland campsite,

Eldoret, Kenya*

Glass*

Corkscrew*

Keep going

Lady

Left

Let's have a baby

Lions

Love you too

Light off

OK*

Try*

Manifest*

Me*

Might be

Mo fia

Money

Music gives

Natures symphony

No doubt

Oh Mother Earth

Ariel view of Scotland

One way

Pay out

Poverty

Pussy

Quote by Rael

CD cover David Nicoll and friends Vol 1* Internet photo

CD cover David Nicoll and friends Vol 2* Internet photo

CD cover David Nicoll and friends Vol 3* Internet photo

Lawn

Mugdog castle outside Glasgow, photo by Gordon Bulman*

Reciting poetry at The Clutha bar, Glasgow, photo by Johnny Cypher*

Fisherman's Blues, photo by Jammy, somewhere off the Butt of Lewis*

The Seer* self portrait

Training*

K9*

Reminiscing again*

Only toking*

Once*

Indeed*

Let it pass*

Rainbow nation

Refuse

Right

Sale

Second hand store

Shit

Sun*

Sublime*

The dark*

Scotts*

Teeth*

Seeing*

Scotsmen (Dramatic)

Seeing you

Shapes

Sheep

Situation

So far away

Something back

Spare

You go*

Might not be so clear*

Would you help me?*

Tranquility*

To the great white hunters, illustration by Jeff Holbrook

View

Wave

Weekend

Where I am

Wife

Wishes

Words

Wouldn't you?

Xenophobia

Yogi tea poetic symphony

Poetry and photograpic collaborations between Tomislav Svorinic and David Nicoll.
RIP Tomi my friend.

Again (for the people of Knysna)

Behind

State capture gives me the blues

I wish

Random photos from my past:

With Mark Whitby and Tomislav Svorniic at Tapas, Hillcrest, South Africa.

Chicken and egg situation

Dana bay sunset,

Knysna poets flyer, photograph by Pierre Opperman

Shaka, the Lady and the Mistress, my djembe drums built by Keith Roderick

Photo taken outside the black house at The Irie eyrie, Bothas hill, South Africa.

With Patricia and Charlene Stutser at Southern Cross music festival, Mooi river.

Eye to eye with Steve Newman, photograph by Shakeenah

A bird in the hand, photograph by Shakeenah, taken in Mossel bay, South Africa

Been to gym photo by Shakeenah

US (United Souls) at Southern Cross music festival, Mooi river, South Africa, 2000

Photo by Erika van Zyl

This is US, Shakeenah, Gary Barker, Nigel Hartman and David at La Peron, Mossel bay

Buck relaxing on the back lawn, Lake Brenton, Knysna, South Africa

International Who's Who of Poetry award, 2012

A solution!

"I need to be free!"

Who is ever free?

Between you or me?

All with previous conditioning,

Upbringing,

Religious conditioning!

Sometimes with,

Sometimes without a honey!

On the Ferris wheel

To survive and prosper!

Everyone now has to

Make money!

Expanding the economy!

Everything alive or dead,

Plant, animal, mineral

Or human!

Is now a commodity!

A commodity!

With a worth in monetary terms!

What is that

To the Universe?

Ultimately for the

Love of money and greed!

Certainly not for need!

What the future holds

We shall see?

As the years go by

Many less species we will see!

Blindfolded by a controlled

Media and press!

Quite a mess!

Conditioning public opinion

With contrived harmony!

Sport "E Sport" in Greek

An escape from reality!

With the planet in monetary terms

In debt!

To who?

Or what?

That I cannot see!

Maybe

Time to check out

A balance!

A status quo?

A common denominator

To maintain our evolution!

Our revolution?

To maintain

Our inheritance

Please God

Provide

A solution!

About you!

"I think that

You have a problem!

I honestly do!"

I replied

"Hello my name is David!

And in fact

That is true!

I have more than one!

How about you?"

Again!

"I am going to miss you!"

"I know, I know!"

As your eyelids fill

And tears gently flow!

"Hambe kahle

Till we meet again!"

May your heart be

Filled with love

And very little strain!

It is never easy to leave

First greeting and then parting

Bound for the Western Cape

Where new music scenes I am starting!

Stay well my lady

May your life be

Full of gain!

Hambe Kahle

One more

Till we meet

Again!

And Harmony!

Just wondering about Cecil's carcass

Was it just skinned, beheaded and left to lie?

From magnificence and pride!

To twisted muscle, raw meat,

Now eaten by others

Including millions of flies!

Not worthless though

If you come back later

And pick up the bones!

Then send them Asian bound!

Within six months,

They will be sold,

Made into Tiger bone wine

And in bottles be found!

This is crazy!

A demand for them

Is around!

Worth more dead than alive!

Fifty thousand dollars

Was paid, Cecil to kill!

Taxidermy fees, transportation

Plus the return to another!

A bone dealer/skeleton stealer!

Who does not care!

That the Lion

Is now still!

Why is every single thing

On this earth now a commodity?

Preserve our wildlife and environment

For future generations to see

Hopefully

In peace, love

And

Harmony!

And rhyme!

Sitting by the peaceful ocean,

The waves lapping gently on the shore!

Sun sinking its last rays,

As the end comes to one

Of those glorious African days!

My lady playing piano beside me!

As a new cell phone app!

Playing the keyboard

On the touch screen

With cellphone

On her lap!

Thank you lord for these

Magic moments in time!

In beauty with nature,

In love, rhythm

And rhyme!

Written on the quay and Kaai 4, Mossel bay

Annual Holiday!

With the second best climate

In the world and the Whales

On their way!

To calve and breed

At Dana bay on their

Annual

Holiday!

Arranges!

The writing as I can see it

Is on the wall!

Everything changes!

What is life?

But experiences,

Friendships!

Lovers!

Stages!

Time and reality

Re arranges!

As mine!

How strange it is through life's different stages!

And how some people can test your limits

To test your ability to avoid rages!

Two separate man

Felt my ladies ass

In different bars!

In my earlier years

They would very shortly thereafter

Have been viewing stars!

The first one

An older gentleman

Dancing round so sweet!

Had a feel while

She was sitting

Him spinning

On his feet!

Bit shocked when I said to him

"You touch my ladies ass again

And we have a problem!" I said!

While he wandered away

Shaking his head!

"I am a good man!"

He did sigh!

My reply being

"So am I!"

Then we get taken out

The next night but late!

To somewhere we could

"Sing our songs!

I am sure it will be great!"

But great it wasn't!

That is for sure!

When we walked in

And saw "Hells Razors!"

On the back of a big guys

Leather jacket!

I thought Trouble, for sure!

He had grabbed her ass within

Two minutes of us coming in!

Shakeenah started shouting and cursing!

Then the two female bikers closed in!

They were big and heavy, aggressive!

Not weak and thin!

He then turned his angry gaze

With eyes of red!

Long pointy brown beard

Aggressive, angry, shouting!

Out of his head!

"Let's get the hell

Out of here!"

I said!

Are we going to the wrong places?

Is what I did think

Realizing that socializing

Is a problem sometime's

When connected with drink!

But she has a lovely ass!

That is for sure!

Visualizing, anticipating,

Desire, hormonal!

No cure!

But all in all

It worked out all fine!

And for the two of you cheapskates

F#ck you! Her ass is where it should be!

In a hand known as mine!

Attack!

The heat has now started,

The summer is now here!

Time to change from

The winter clothes

Into the lightweight gear!

Went for a smoke this morning

At the smoking shed!

Sat on the wooden bench

Then "What is that?"

Hugh he said!

I looked down to my right

And there on the floor

Was a fully grown puff adder

Minus its head!

"Oh God!"

I thought

And jumped to the side!

Panic biting me

Deep inside!

What a fright

Really not good crack!

That sight is enough

To give someone

A heart attack!

BUTTERFLY

As I said before,
We are like butterflies,
Flying together
While we choose!
Sometimes taking
Erratic and exciting
Pathways, at other times
A cruise!

There comes a time
For both of us to say,
From now on
We will fly,
Our individual way,

A time for change
It leaves a sigh,
We flew some
Beautiful flights
Together
Dear Butterfly!

Butt!

Daisy the goat
Had a heart of gold
And with horses and dogs
Was ever so bold!

Her head in the horse food bucket
Did not please the pawing mare,
As Daisy's tail is held high up,
Chomping, without a care.

Then rascal the wiry
Terrier would come
Nipping at her legs
Without leaving a cut,
Then she would rear up
And proceed to
Crash down
Trying to give the dog
A head butt!

Bay!

Sunday afternoon 5pm! At Bushbuck camp, Sedgefield,
Western Cape, South Africa!

We are so loathe

To leave this sanctuary!

Birds chirping, sun setting!

But we have to flee!

Back to Mossel bay

By the clear blue sea!

But when we arrive

It's down to Kaai 4!

Where I can finish off

This perfect weekend once more!

How can I put this?

What can I say?

I am going back

To jump in the Ocean

And float

In Mossel bay!

Be you!

What a conundrum!

What a stew!

Half the people want to

Shag you!

The other half

Want to *Moer you!

This is true!

And when the first half

Find that they can't

Shag you!

They want to

Moer you too!

Shakeenah

Such is your

Beauty and appeal!

Just continue

To

Be you!

*Moer = Hit

Being sown!

The world controlled!

Force fed on GMOs and other toxins

With little that we can do!

Sweeteners, meat, chicken,

Milk and water too!

How can things have

Changed in a matter

Of centuries?

A blink in the eye

Of momentary time!

Where a corporation!

A non-entity actually!

Only ink on paper!

Can poison and control seed

Solely for profits and greed!

A machine!

Not in our favorite dream!

Bringing damage to the planet

And its citizens too!

Creating some irreversible damage

But with the politicians bought,

Laws passed,

Gazetted and approved!

What can you do?

Seeds now a valuable commodity!

With one corporation Monsanto!

An immoral profit driven entity!

Creating damage and wanting to control

Our food supply

Indefinitely!

The future...

To control the people

Control the food supply!

This could be our ultimate destiny!

Minimizing competition!

No growing your own!

A monster has been hatched

From one man's mind

And its seeds are now

Being sown!

CHUGGA CHUG

Chugga chug, chugga chug,
Chugga chug, chugga chug,
With clouds of steam
Pumping out in a flowing trail,
The ancient train
Climbs up the mountainside track,
As to the grey clouds above,
The condensing water
Does slowly sail.

From times gone by
Now past history,
Steam engines have
Now been relegated
To near obscurity,
Mainly pictures in books
For your children to see.

Nations were developed
And criss crossed by
These engineering dreams,
How great now to hear
The chugga chugga
Chugga chugga and
Its whistle blowing
With high pitched
Screams!

COMPARE

alert and aware,
temporary face painting,
no limitations,
nothing to
compare!

Designs!

The moth takes a rest
Atop the sunscreens
Fine patterned lines
It is not difficult
To see where some
Of our jet designers
Copied
Nature's
Wing
Designs!

DOUBT

waiting
feeling
the silky web
the spider hangs
upside down
fangs curled out,
this photo will
scare some
of that
i have
no
doubt!

Bad taste!

"I hope you don't leave us!"

Said an Englishman to me!

Scottish referendum coming up,

The results for the world to see!

"We love the bagpipes

And we actually quite like you!"

He honestly said that!

This story is true!

So not to disappoint him

And make his comments a waste!

I said "Well, I can't put you down

For bad taste!"

Breakfast!

Does your lady

Take long while getting ready

To go out for a meal?

Mine does

As by this statement,

You will feel!

Tired of waiting,

My patience at its last

"Don't worry baby,

No rush!

We will just go

For breakfast!

TREAT IT SO !

A POETIC AND MUSICAL COLLABORATION
BY
MERVYN FULLER
AND
DAVID NICOLL

THE BUT 'N BEN

Cheaper!

"It will be much better if you shop alone!"

She said!

Couldn't be sweeter!

Then she said!

"It will also be

Much cheaper!"

Cocktails!

So Scotland just lost

A cricket game against

Afghanistan!

The wind now

Out of their sails!

Mind you,

These Afghanis

Have been practicing for years

By throwing grenades

And Molotov

Cocktails!

BOO!

Children play
As only children do
While Paul shows us
How to
Peek a boo!

His neck!

There is nothing wrong with my ass!

She said while loosening some phlegm!

"I know, that is the problem!

It is like an eye magnet!

For those with eyes!

Normally eliciting

Painful groins or even

From women some sighs!

So glad that you are mine!

The future looking fine!

Sipping on some Rose wine!

What the hell!

What the heck!

Must say I do feel sorry for the poor guy

Who accidentally

Sprained

His neck!"

BY

slicing through
the sky,
the colours fly,
a rainbow
signifying
that the storm
has
passed
by!

Booze!

This is some situation

One which I did not choose,

A father who asks me money for rent arrears,

Mother wants money for gambling

And sister wants money

For booze!

Brother!

This is one example why you shouldn't deal in stolen goods!

It can come back on you or your brood!

A father ordered a cheap BMW from hijackers!

They got him one but ultimately

He got a kick in the knackers!

Ordered it as a present for his daughters

Twenty first birthday!

Two years later his son is

Now wanting the same

As it was now his twenty first birthday!

So the father in Johannesburg

Ordered another BMW,

Just the same as the other!

His daughter was shot in a hijacking

And her car taken

To be given

To her

Younger

Brother!

For the Rhinos and for the attention of the users of Rhino horn.

This is written for the ancient superstitious minds that are

Creating the decimation of a species and specifically for the users of Rhino horn.

Spread it far and wide so that maybe, just maybe,

They might think again about what they are doing!

You never know, maybe after reading this poem one,

Just one person might think about what he is doing and change his mind.

Then the next time that he gets offered some,

He will refuse and when asked why?

Explain to his friends his reasons and then they in turn

Might also think again about what they are doing.

We must try to nullify the demand

Regardless of how massive a task this may seem to be.

I have had this poem translated into Chinese and Vietnamese

So that we can actually get some users of Rhino horn to read it.

I would appreciate it if you could either send it to contacts in

China or Vietnam or alternatively send me suggestions

As to who would be the right people to send it to

So that we might get through to them and I will send it to them.

I have already sent it out to newspapers etc over there but let's

Actually get it through to them so that logic,

Reason and compassion might break through to them and make a difference.

I see the Rhino poaching situation as a thorn bush with many branches,

When you catch some poachers you break off a branch but the branch

Will soon grow again.

What we need to do is drill a hole into the root of the bush

And spread the poison in the roots itself.

We can but try and your help would be appreciated.

Captivity!

So you think that

Rhino horn cures cancer?

I find that difficult to see,

And there is absolutely no

Proof of this medically!

Still in your belief of this

You keep trying

And you,

Like the Rhino

Are still dying!

Even if it worked

As a temporary cure,

You are still

Going to die,

That is for sure!

So a species is being

Exterminated

As to your God

You pray,

Ignorant,

Or uncaring

Of the Rhino's

Final day!

Then there are the ones

Who have a belief

That it will turn you on,

To lift your dick up

An aphrodisiac!

Oh man,

You have problems,

Try Viagra,

Or visualize

Whatever

Turns you on!

The truth is

That it does

NONE of these!

It is superstition

And ancient beliefs,

Never stated

Or used by any

African chiefs!

All Rhino horn is,

Is Keratin,

The same as your

Nails and hair!

But because of

Misguided Eastern

Beliefs a species

Is threatened

With possible

Extermination!

Dagger handles

Is also another use

For Arab sheiks

Who are out on the loose,

Lots of money

Very little strain,

With oil wealth,

They like the

Expensive horn

As it has a

Nice grain,

But will the Rhino

Ever recover

From this onslaught

Once again?

The only way to

Stop this slaughter

Is to nullify the demand!

By education

And conservation,

Or maybe your children

Might find it difficult

To understand,

How a majestic animal

Who once roamed

Wide and free

Has now been annihilated

And is only

Pictures in books

For them to see!

Apart from some

Precious specimens

In Zoo's,

In captivity!

CDs!

Calum my friend!

We have travelled many roads together,

In Scotland and Canada

We were into a good time!

Meeting new friends

And having a blether!

As fate would have it

At this moment

You have released a new CD!

Well done! Can you please send me a copy?

Would love to hear it and where

You are coming from!

In your own unique style of rhythm,

Melody and song!

I return I shall send to you!

"David Nicoll and friends, Volume two!"

Had to change it a bit, wee copyright issue,

Which was not much fun!

So I dropped the tracks with my friend Steve Newman

And put in tracks by MAD Mervyn And Dave

And am in the process right now

Of releasing it as Volume two (Rev 1)

When the Calleoch's get to hear them

They will be clapping their knees!

Saying "Look at these two Bottoch's

Both in their sixties

And still releasing CDs!"

Calleoch's = old women in Gaelic

Bottoch's = old men in Gaelic

Coin!

You cannot criticize anything Jewish
Without being classified and labeled
As anti Semitic!
Which many have found as the after effects
Have made them sick!

You cannot criticize anything Islamic!
Without risking being classified and labeled
As Islamophobic!
The after effects of this
Can also make you sick!

So strange, once brothers!
Living in land together
They did join!
Now these two extremes are merely
Two sides of the
Same coin!

Daddy!

Forgive me my daughter

For whatever it may be?

Why do you no longer contact me?

I still love you!

Don't you see?

Don't be influenced against me

By stories from your Mummy!

Divorce nowadays

Is just a stage!

Happens to lots of people

Whatever their age!

Call me sometime

Or come and see?

You're ever loving

And lonesome

Daddy!

Written for Gordon Bulman

Do You!

"I am sorry that I get

On your tit's sometimes baby!

I am used to living alone!

A complex character

That is true!

But I do also love

Getting on your tit's

At other loving times

And so

Do you!"

.

Fire

the skirl o the pipes
the foottapping beat
the piper
immaculate,
extremely
neat.

playing
amazing grace,
loch lomond and
mull of kintyre
with my hair
standing up,
heart and soul
on
fire!

DRUNKEN DRIVING

Does the road look like this,
When you drive home at night,
Have you been drinking?
Are you feeling alright?
Stop, think! Don't drink and drive.
Save the accident, stay alive!
As a test of sobriety,
Close one of your eyes,
Are there still two lines?
Are you wise?
Please, sleep by the way,
And forget about your ego's size.

Charlene

such a pretty show
of petals,
rarely to be seen,
two of us,
Patricia and
Charlene!

Poetic licence

SCOTTISH POET,
MUSICIAN AND
WOLF-LOVER DAVID
NICOLL RETAINS
MORE THAN A
LITTLE OF HIS
VIKING HERITAGE,
AS SALLY SCOTT
DISCOVERED

I HAVE a feeling that David Nicoll, the KZN poet/musician who dances around his abode with his own pack of wolves, may be a throwback to some wild and inimitable Viking ancestor...

The Scotsman, originally from the ancient Viking settlement of Stornoway on the Outer Hebrides Isle of Lewis, is one of those multi-talented, off-the-wall types who defy category.

This father of three (his adult children live and work overseas) may list his day job as professional draughtsman, but he is also a wandering minstrel, poet and djembe drummer, whose illustrated book *Thoughts and Reflections* offers everything from the meditative to brooding and bawdy.

As a "poet first and foremost", David has been writing for around 25 years, often using djembe drumming and music to accompany his poetry. "It

adds another dimension – gets the words out to a much larger audience."

In KwaZulu-Natal, David is a regular performer, from the annual Splashy Fen Music Festival to Durban's Live Poets Society. His reputation has also spread beyond these shores. In 1997, chosen for a group of "International Poets of Merit", he spent a week in Washington DC, conversing with like-minded souls, and making it to the semi-finals of this prestigious competition.

One of David's poems, *Indeed*, is a short ode to "a statesman to the world" Nelson Mandela. A thank you letter from the Office of the president records how "inspired" Mandela was by the piece David sent to him.

Being a maverick, not surprisingly, David's home in Scotland was one of his many jobs. His own "castle" in lurks in the depths of Strangsend.

His Hobbit-style "livingwall" home, built with maximum regard for the environment, nestles against a hillside with a view over a fabulous valley. He likes to be "close to nature", hence this low-impact abode, created eight years ago via the "cut-and-fill" excavation method, using materials found on the land.

The combined stone-walled living room, bedroom and kitchen includes a sack-walled shower and wood-fired stove. A light, airy guest bedroom has a large bed and bath.

Outside is an aviary, veggie patch and orchard full of lemons, pawpaws, avocados, limes, litchies and oranges.

"Scottish by birth, African by choice", David came here in 1982. Having met an "unhappy, homesick" South African while working in chilly Grangemouth in Scotland. "He was living there because his Scottish wife had wanted to come

home, and he turned me with tales of sun, sea and pools in back gardens! My mates thought I was crazy, but I decided to go to South Africa."

Nowadays, David keeps house with a lively pack of wolves, bought from a specialist breeder and named Snow, Shadow, Prince, Princess and Pretty Boy.

When this boisterous bunch lope towards you on masse it is, initially, perturbing, but the mutual love affair between poet and pack is obvious, and they do tend to keep the baddies at bay.

Is David happy with life? "Pretty much, as long as I can go on writing and performing with friends."

Meanwhile, there is another odd abode... "One day I want to return to the tree-house, the Bath Ben I built at the Ndaleni coastal campsite, near Eldoret in the Kenyan Highlands. It was built on three-metre poles next to a river, so peaceful and close to nature. Peaceful, rather like the large wolf, which, as we speak, lies asleep on his foot. C

Day!

What an ironic situation!

Bringing my boss

Very little cheer!

Now the tables have turned

And it is him

And not us that lives in fear!

That was the way he used to rule!

Control freak and instilling

Fear and insecurity!

Really not cool!

It used to honestly

Get to me!

The insecurity!

Now the tables have turned

I no longer fear

Being burned!

The company now talking

About cutting back staff

By forty percent!

Quite a toll,

Which means that about

Seven hundred heads

Are going to roll!

"I am too young to retire!

Don't want to move to Joburg or Durban!"

He was heard to say!

Well, maybe one day?

He will have no say?

Poetic justice I have found

Is that what goes around,

Comes around!

What will happen?

Who can say?

I am just going

To take this

Day by

Day!

Desire!

Desire!

The spark to make things happen

That is true!

If you don't have desire

For something or someone

There is little that you can do!

Desire!

The want, the need

Like a fresh summer shower!

Ignites your mind and

Emerges as willpower!

Chorus:

Desire! Desire!

Chase what you aspire!

Set your heart on fire!

Desire!

Without it there would be

No progress or development!

Imagination creates desire

As if heaven sent!

Desire!

Is Universal although residing

In your heart and mind!

Desire! Can be for personal gain

Or to help the poor, the sick, the homeless,

The deaf or the blind!

Chorus

Desire!

Can be for others or for

Personal creativity or gain!

Desire! Can be for something transforming!

That you might be born again!

Desire!

Has no limitations,

It is truly free!

Desire!

Is a blessing bestowed

On humanity!

Chorus

Instrumental and end!

Die!

"We should drill and inject deadly poison

Inside all living Rhino horn!"

Wayne did sigh!

"Then tell all the poachers

And users

If you use this

You are going

To die!"

Do me!

"I am cold now!"

"Oh, you do look a bit Holey

Right enough!"

Very stylish,

A lady like this I never met!

As she was wearing a very

Shapely fishing net!

Now I was a fisherman

And this appeals to me!

As apart from her

Beautiful body,

Right through it

I did see!

Which was quite appealing

And crazy!

Now this lady is fine, cultured!

A real dish!

The only things that I ever saw

In a fishing net were dead sheep

And lots of fish!

I didn't mean she was getting religious,

Although high spiritually!

She has just shown me

That you can be Holey

And free!

Incidentally, dear lady!

You will do me!"

Earnings!

"Here is some money

Keep an eye on her,

Make sure that she is OK!"

This is what the skipper did say!

"Here is some money!"

To Rodwyn, Sharee did also say!

Must have made his day!

Lessened his yearnings

And also

Doubled

His

Earnings!

Escape!

Made a statement

Found it difficult to escape!

"You know that being with you,

I must be the luckiest man

In the Western Cape!"

"Only the Western Cape?"

Was her

Escape!

Face!

"I don't want to be famous!"

"Me neither!"

"You would have no freedom left!

People would be hassling you everywhere!

"You would never get a breather!

"No more walking the street anonymously!

As everyone would have seen

Your face on TV!"

Couldn't just walk into any bar

Or restaurant, it wouldn't be sweet!"

You couldn't even scratch your ass

While walking in the street!"

"Your photo would be in the newspapers

And lots of magazines!"

"Your sexual preferences, partners

And peccadilloes,

Would be described and debated

In many different scenes!"

"Better to be infamous!

It is absolutely no disgrace!

As lots of people

Have heard about you!

But not many

Know your

Face!"

Few!

"Dave!" the boss said!

"I think that you have a problem!"

And I agree this is true!

"Booze is one!

But there are

Another

Few!"

Feeds you!

I just had five hundred rand

Transferred from my bank account!

To e wallet without my knowing!

"Who did that?"

My suspicions no growing!

Could it be the same one

That increased my daily withdrawal limit

To seven thousand rand?

Many seeds this person is sowing!

Previously, a long list to see!

Of twenty six withdrawals

To convert from airtime

To data for free!

Without my knowledge

But who pays for it?

Me!!!

This happens to be the lady

Who holds my hand!

The data withdrawals amounted to

Two and a half thousand rand!

Almost beyond belief!

I am obviously entangled

With a thief!

"I love you dear sir"

"I love you too!"

But you are

Biting the hand

That

Feeds you!

For Free!

Coming up to Xmas time!

For everyone a time of good cheer!

With happiness, gifts, presents,

Champagne, wine, good food and beer!

But in holiday resorts around

The South African coast!

A situation arises

Which is nothing about

Which we can boast!

All the prices go up

For everything!

Food, booze, accommodation,

Gifts, presents!

As the till bells

Constantly ring!

This to the business owners

Much happiness and profit

Does this bring!

The locals get left

With their backs to the wall!

As they just can't afford

The inflated prices

Until after the tourists

Have left and then

All the prices will fall!

With the rand being so low!

It brings extreme irony!

As life is South Africa

For the locals is

Extremely expensive!

But for all the foreign tourists

Everything here

Is almost

For free!

For sure!

She had "Ingrid Jonkeritis!"

Is what I say!

As on the eighteenth of August 2014!

At Santos beach in Mossel bay!

Early evening, lost, hopeless, depressed!

She walked into the waves, to stay!

But things were not meant to be that way!

As a security guard saw her and shouted

"Are you OK?"

This changed her mind set, broke her focus!

She turned around from the sea

And walked away!

Later that evening around about eight!

A meeting was destined!

What can be described by both of US

As fate!

I was also at that time depressed!

Without car!

Stuck in Mossel bay!

I could not go far!

I go to "The trap!" a coloured bar

Where I had never been before!

Having a quiet beer, checking out the high pitched

And excited conversations around me!

You know the score!

Then something happened

Which changed our future

When we met face to face!

Both exuberant, excited

Spirits flighted!

Souls ignited!

We both knew

This is US!

For sure!

Forty nine!

Wanted to buy a fountain pen!

Went into a fancy store!

They wanted three thousand rand for one!

"I am not paying that!"

You know the score!

But today,

I walked into a Crazy store!

Writing this poem

In rhythm, metre and rhyme!

In a fountain pen

With four nibs

And ink colours

That cost

Forty nine!

Forty nine!

Frustrated!

"Whatever you do, there are consequences!"

Mervyn did say! How true!

There is no escaping that

From either me or you!

What you say!

What you do!

Determines in the mirror!

The reflection, action, compassion!

Happiness and joy!

For just being alive in harmony and peace!

Scenting the fresh air

As a young boy!

What an extreme pleasure!

Fresh sea air in my lungs!

Inspired! Rejuvenated!

No more

Frustrated!

Fun!

I come in

It is only candles on!

Is it load shedding again?

Or is my lady

Wanting

Some fun?

Go!

"What is the time baby?"

My lady wanted to know!

I told her

"I have been waiting for ages

It is

Time

To go!"

Happy day?

A workmate just turned sixty today!

"Happy birthday to you!"

At the smoke hut I did say!

He was a bit deflated!

Not full of the usual fire!

And was wondering

"What will I do

When I retire?"

"Maybe I will get a backie

And move people's furniture?

Don't want to just sit at home

And vegetate!

That is for sure!"

"Look on the bright side,

Retirement is only sixty months away!"

To cheer him up

I did say!

"With you being staff and having

A month's holiday a year

That leaves only fifty five months work left

Does that not bring good cheer?"

"Only two hundred and twenty

Weeks at work left!"

But still he looked bereft!

"That is only eleven hundred

Working days left!"

"That is all

That lies in store!

Then after that,

You need never see

Your disliked boss

Anymore!"

I know that with age

Your hair turns grey!

But it is that not going to be

A

Happy day?

Dave!

"I think that I just shouted out Jesus!

When you put it in!"

"The passion I could not save!"

I then replied

"No, it is not him,

It is me,

Dave!"

FUN

"Hello!"
I heard from the car,
Looked in,
Couldn't see anyone.
Then up pops this
Young lad's face
Full of energy,
Excitement
    And
    Fun!

EVIL!

The cape glossy starling,
Flying free as she will,
Perched on the back
Of a wooden chair
Looking positively
Evil!

Everyone!

"I am on!"

She said in fun!

"Oh, OK!

But don't show

Everyone!"

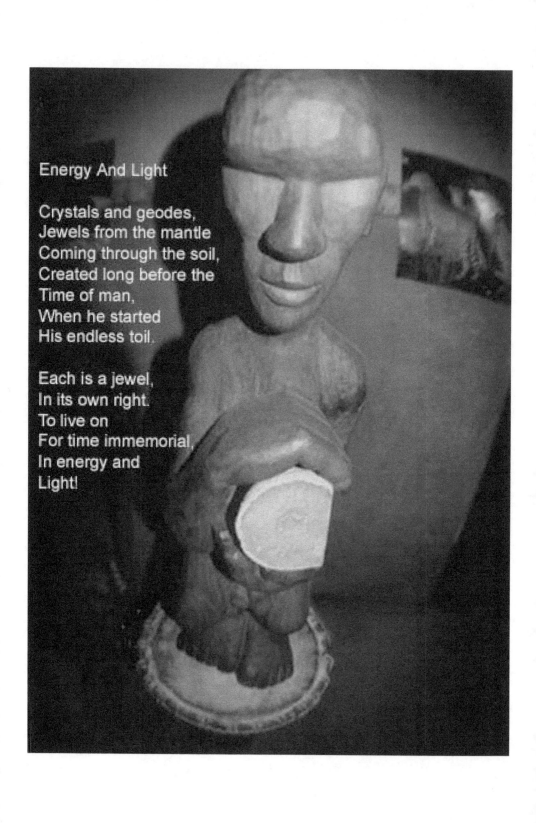

Energy And Light

Crystals and geodes,
Jewels from the mantle
Coming through the soil,
Created long before the
Time of man,
When he started
His endless toil.

Each is a jewel,
In its own right.
To live on
For time immemorial,
In energy and
Light!

HEAD

Suspended
As if a
Spider's thread,
The backlit
Mesh hanging
From the red hammock
A fine place
To rest
Your
Head!

Hear And See!

Nothing like you!

There is nothing or no one like you!

You are so unique and special!

I am in love with you!

You sing, you rhyme

In harmony and melody!

Totally sublime!

Dancing so free

With life in creativity

And poetic harmony!

You are free!

You are free!

Free in Spirit,

Free in Soul!

Creating your destiny

For all ultimately

To hear

And see!

"Hi Steve!"

I have this poem that works so well with your song called At Nix!

Could I possibly record over it, it is brilliant, No Tricks!"

"That sounds great!" he replied, it did not put him to task!

Then he added, "You don't even have to ask!"

"I do my friend; otherwise it would not be right!

But thank you for your permission

It is sure to bring some light!"

This conversation happened Pinetown at the Rainbow revue bar!

Where he was performing with Lu Dlamini, another African singing star!

Madala Kunene was also there and Guy Buttery too!

The same day that Madala and myself decided that we now both had time

And new music and poetry we would now do!

In years ago, it was well over two!

So into my friends Steve Cresswell's studio I did go!

With Steve Newman's CD playing in the background

Giving a lovely flow!

Then my imagination started to go!

And another poetic musical combination

Started to grow!

Not intentional, but a Spiritual flow!

"What we leave behind!

Came in with another track,

Flowing in synch

All the time!

Only two of us in the studio!

Everything working out fine!

Nothing planned with only one track

In my mind!

But then my Spirit and

Some of the other tracks did flow!

This was not my intention

I would like you to know!

It was total freewheeling

Words and music combine!

To give freewheeling thoughts

And music to feel fine

So that is the way that it did go!

I was just going with the flow!

It was serendipitous

That it should work out this way!

And that I should be standing in front of you today!

With a copyright infringement

Charge against me!

I did not plan this!

It was meant to be!

Steve Newman and myself

Are old soul brothers

I apologize for any

Inconvenience caused!

This was an experimental

CD never released!

Or will be using

The peace of Eden tracks

So fine me

What you will

And then

Relax!

Hold my hand!

Original lyrics mixed in with Michael Jackson and Akon's song!

Hold my hand!

Hold my hand!

Now we live in Mossel bay,

Sometimes life here is difficult to understand,

If we walk through this place hand in hand!

Because there are still some racists around here

Who just don't understand!

Ooh, what the hell, I just say

Hold my hand!

Hold my hand!

Baby I promise that I will do all I can!

Hold my hand!

Things will get better if you,

Hold my hand!

Hold my hand!

The nights are getting darker!

And there's no peace inside!

So why make life harder

Why don't you just

Hold my hand

Hold my hand!

Baby I promise I'll do all I can!

Hold my hand

Hold my hand!

He said!

Dancing around freely

On the white tiled floor!

Shakeenah kicked a bottle,

An accident, you know the score!

Now Dave the poet

Couldn't miss out on this

Opportunity to write a POKE

And create some bliss!

Immediately after,

A thought came to his head!

"You are lucky that it wasn't a bucket!"

He said!

Honestly!

What a situation!

Quite a scene!

Involved with three women

At the same time!

No physically

But emotionally

If you know what I mean!

Ultimately costly!

In one form or another!

Keeping on the road the show!

To develop and grow!

Life is interesting!

That much I know!

But this is Africa!

And sometimes

That is the way

That it

Does flow!

The future?

Que Sera Sera!

What will be will be

I am in love! Honestly!

I am too!

Went to see Piet Botha and the Lyzyrd Kyngs

At La Peron in Mossel bay just yesterday!

They were brilliant I must say!

Spoke to him later, swapped CDs and some wit!

But this Monday morning, I am in the shit!

I should really just have stayed in bed!

Drank too much and the alcohol tester at the gate turned red!

Then off to another room for a second test!

Even after drinking lots of water, eating a sausage roll,

It was still over! Feel I just need some rest!

Another six men there! One small African man

Who stood straight as a rod!

Blew zero point zero!

The security guard asked him

"Who are you? He replied

"I am a son of God!"

So now I sit pondering my fate,

Waiting for the reading to go below the legal limit

Then I will drive home to see my female mate!

My boss was not happy, that is true!

Ending his shitting out session with

"I am disappointed in you!"

Well, if the truth be known,

I suppose that

I am too!

It up!

"The ice is cold in here!"

Said Alan shaking

The red wine

In the old tin cup!

"If I was you would go

And complain

And ask them to

Heat it up!"

I mean!

"Have you had a drink today?"

To Shakeenah I did say!

"I had two ciders

To help me clean the flat

And wash the floor

With a musical sway!"

"Oh well,

I suppose that is OK!"

"Everything is sparkling and clean

And if all it cost

Is two ciders

Then it is well

Worth it!

Know what I mean?"

In tears!

The tusks get smuggled in boxes!

The calves the same way too!

Separated from their mothers and herds,

To end up in a foreign zoo!

Africa's wildlife is all heading East!

And watch is all the rest of the world

Cares to do!

What wildlife will be left in Africa

In thirty years?

Not much for sure!

This will leave many

In tears!

Into the future!

Into the future with eyes wide open,

Into the future with wishes and hoping!

Into the future in every nation!

Into the future with innovation and creation!

Into the future in peace and harmony!

Into the future daily sunrise to see!

Into the future to look after the Earth!

Into the future our home for all its worth!

Into the future with Spirits flying!

Into the future to cease pain and crying!

Into the future positively trying!

Into the future loving one another!

Into the future all humanity, sister and brother!

Into the future no looking back!

Into the future balanced on track!

Into the future caring and sharing!

Into the future with compassion not staring!

Into the future in love with your honey!

Into the future not making a God of money!

Into the future on this beautiful unique spot!

Into the future on this precious blue dot!

It Go!

"Control yourself David!"

I thought while going with the flow!

Sharon replied

"No!!!

Let it go!"

It!

"I really don't fancy another beer!"

But then again this is causing me strain!

If I don't drink it now,

It won't be here for much longer!

As you will drink it again!!

This thought

Is giving me shit!

So I have made a decision

I will just

Drink

It!

ANYTHING!

"Oh! What are they?"
The customer asked
The nurseryman
With an inquisitive ring.
"Well, they are all that's
Left of the last
Customer who came
And didn't buy
Anything!"

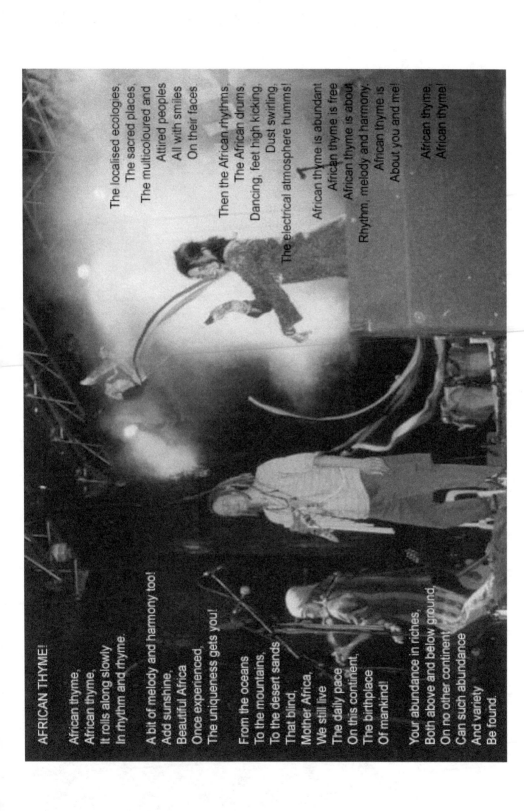

AFRICAN THYME!

African thyme,
African thyme,
It rolls along slowly
In rhythm and rhyme.

A bit of melody and harmony too!
Add sunshine.
Beautiful Africa
Once experienced,
The uniqueness gets you!

From the oceans
To the mountains,
To the desert sands.
That blind,
Mother Africa.
We still live
The daily pace
On this continent,
The birthplace
Of mankind!

Your abundance in riches,
Both above and below ground,
On no other continent
Can such abundance
And variety
Be found.

The localised ecologies,
The sacred places,
The multicoloured and
Attired peoples
All with smiles
On their faces.

Then the African rhythms.
The African drums,
Dancing, feet high kicking,
Dust swirling,
The electrical atmosphere humms!

African thyme is abundant
African thyme is free
African thyme is about
Rhythm, melody and harmony,
African thyme is
About you and me!

African thyme.
African thyme!

Awesome!

Shongweni, Awesome Africa Festival,
Rich cultures of note,
With a multi coloured audience,
Of its richness and ambiance
Lots will quote.

The music, the vibe,
The quality, the drive,
So awesome to be here,
To be alive!

The poets, with their wisdom,
Running through their genes,
The sangomas dazzling beadwork,
Traditional healers,
Environmental greens.

Something really unique
Is happening here,
A statement to the world,
By its interracial harmony
And abundant good cheer.

This unique event
With cultures many
And diverse,
Is not only an example
To the planet,
But the whole universe!

GLASS

Got a Christmas present
From Greg my mate,
It was in a homemade
Red Christmas stocking
Until Christmas day,
I did wait.

I pulled out a box.
It is a
Personal Penis enlarger.
I was wondering
"Is it like a suction tube
Or maybe an
Electric charger?"

"Guaranteed
To work on all sizes!"
The advertising pass.
I then opened it up
To find....
A magnifying
Glass!

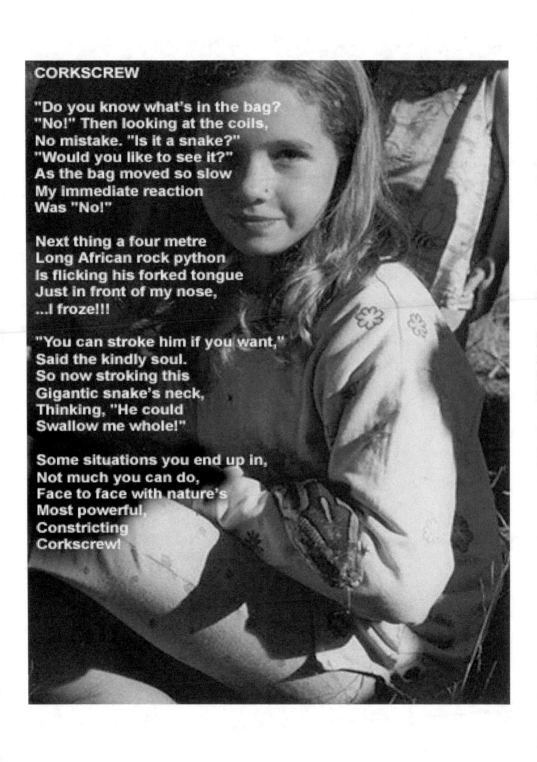

CORKSCREW

"Do you know what's in the bag?
"No!" Then looking at the coils,
No mistake. "Is it a snake?"
"Would you like to see it?"
As the bag moved so slow
My immediate reaction
Was "No!"

Next thing a four metre
Long African rock python
Is flicking his forked tongue
Just in front of my nose,
...I froze!!!

"You can stroke him if you want,"
Said the kindly soul.
So now stroking this
Gigantic snake's neck,
Thinking, "He could
Swallow me whole!"

Some situations you end up in,
Not much you can do,
Face to face with nature's
Most powerful,
Constricting
Corkscrew!

I wish you beauty,
From the flowers
In the spring,
I wish you music,
From the sweet birds
That sing,
I wish you peace,
By the gentle stream,
And guidance
By the spirit
In his ultimate scheme.

I wish you health,
I wish you wealth,
I wish you
Gold in store,
I wish you heaven,
Here on earth,
Now what
Can I wish you more?

Keep going!

Loneliness and depression go hand in hand!

For those not experiencing it,

They find it difficult to understand!

As most sufferers

Were at one time or another in the past

Heart to heart, hand to hand!

Having no barriers between colour or race!

It can take a lot to put a smile on your troubled face!

According to today's Sunday newspaper

It is growing in South Africa at an alarming pace!

With 230 attempted suicides every single day

Twenty three being successful in their mission!

No longer are they on this planet to stay!

My younger brother Derek supposedly did so many years ago!

Aged thirty with still so much of life to go!

Lots live, lots die!

Some despair, some sigh!

But for life and its exuberance

You really must try!

As in the classic statement!

There but for the grace of God go I!

Give me wings and make me fly!

To fulfill my purpose here!

Make people laugh, think, ponder

Or tear running from eye!

Let thy will be done

Under this African sun!

Serendipitous meetings

Sitting on the dock of this bay!

Breezes blowing, seagulls flowing,

An inner vice saying

"Keep going!"

"Keep going!"

Written at Kaai 4, Mossel bay, South Africa, sitting next to the water!

Lady!

On the sixteenth of August

Two thousand and fourteen!

History was about to

Repeat itself!

Although for many

This was unseen!

A lady poet

Walked into the evening waves

In Mossel bay!

Depressed, wanting to go

Into the sea to stay!

A security guard saw her

And gave her a shout,

At this, she thought twice,

Said she was Ok!

And then came out!

Soaken wet,

Lonely and cold!

Still young,

Only thirty years old!

Saved to live more life

In its roller coaster ride!

Saved from a

Watery suicide!

The similarity to be found,

Is with Ingrid Jonker,

Who is no longer around!

Since then she has created,

In poetry, design and song!

With a natural beauty

And kind heart,

Nothing wrong!

As fate would have it,

By pure Serendipity!

We met later that very evening

And I am honoured to say

That she is now

My Lady!

Left!

"Don't use all the data!

I want to SKYPE my daughter tomorrow!"

Shakeenah was playing DVD after DVD

From youtube!

No sign of sorrow!

So now it is New Year's day!

And I am left bereft!

Just loaded three gigs of data

A couple of days ago

And guess what?

No f#ckin data

Left!

Let's have a baby!

Here's one for the soap opera scriptwriters

For their next episode!

They would never think this up!

This is an ode!

"Let's have a baby honey!"

"That would be great!

But could cost a lot of money!"

As my balls have been snipped

Many years ago!

No longer do the

Fertile sperm

Up my penile tube flow!

You say that for you

To have more babies, it is too late!

So we would have to

Find a surrogate!

Take your eggs out

Put them in a petri dish!

Then I could deposit a load

Of fertile sperm

On top of them!

You could give me a hand

If you wish!

Living in Africa

We tend to get a tan!

But anything is possible

At a price

And we can

Makaplan!

Lions!

Lions have been

Turned into the

Equivalent of cattle!

A situation

With no win!

And all for their

Trophies

Bones and skin!

Love you too!

I am truly blessed

To be loved by a lady like you!

You lift my Spirit!

Give me joy,

Warmth, comfort

And stability!

I love you too!

I love you too!

I love you too!

Light off!

"And are there any nice young men for me?"

Asked Myra to Herman, who is Reunion bound!

"Yes, there are many on the island to be found!

But there is only one wee technicality

As she is from South Africa you see!

Where passions are released

For whites only!

"There colour could be a problem!"

He replied modestly!

"Hakuna Matata!" I chirped

Like a real toff!

"If you fancy him,

Just switch the

Light off!"

OK

Used to have three black austropolus hens
And one cockerel, a pleasure to hear
And see
With three large brown eggs supplied daily
Apart from hen food for free!

They roamed free range, clucking.
Shaking earth through their
Blue, green, black glow
Unfortunately now, apart from the cockerel
They are no more, no more movement
No farmyard flow!

Got a three month old puppy
Three months ago
She has created some unseen strain
As one by one
She ate the hens
They will never be again

Instincts inherent
No doubt all in the the DNA
A white wolf's ancestral food
Was chickens, birds,
Anything living, or not,
Which is found
And tasted
Ok!

TRY

sunlight reflecting
from the ocean,
a clear blue sky
highlit clouds
rise from the
horizon
as another
night
eases on
by
a new day
dawns
unlimited potential,
and opportunity
in whatever
you want
to try!

MANIFEST

When seeking inspiration
For something new,
One has to go inside
To find out what to do,
For the inspiration
Is from the spirit
Who inspires
And guides
You through!

When dreaming of the future,
Of things you would like to be,
Your thoughts amass,
Then fly out,
Into universal energy!
Time ticks by whether
At work or at rest,
Until your dream
Becomes.....
Manifest!

Me!

I love my lady

She is so free!

"Even if I am asleep!

You are welcome

To

Disturb

Me!"

Might be!

The thing about anxiety

Is that you worry needlessly!

Living in fear!

Not in good cheer!

Scared of what

Might be!

Mo Fia!

This lady is one

Who has passion and desire!

Ladies and gentlemen

Let me introduce…..

The one and only…..

Mo Fia!!!!!

Written about S.P Lindert

Money!

It was at this very beach

Over twenty five years ago!

 I wrote the poem Man and the Whale here

The sea winds still blow!

Much has changed

In these twenty five years!

For our wildlife, our inheritance

On this earth!

As most of it is being

Decimated in Africa!

The poor animals not

Having a chance!

Our big five

Are in great demand!

For horn, tusk

Or aphrodisiac

In eastern land!

Skins for floors

Trophies for walls!

Some shot like Lions

In canned hunting

Operations!

That doesn't take

Much balls!

We must maintain a balance

In all Ecology!

Wildlife, flora and fauna

A beauty to see!

Natures balance!

Everything having a

Place and time,

Each food source tapped,

All in its season!

Nature's mystery!

Species shrinking in number!

Alarm bells ringing!

While the poachers

And traffickers

Various body parts

Of our wildlife

They are stealing!

Leaving everyone

Who cares reeling!

What are we seeing?

Whole Elephant herds

Mowed down by AK47!

While twelve hundred

Dehorned Rhino

Last year in South Africa,

Went to Rhino heaven!

Canned Lions

A lucrative trade!

With plenty profits

To be made!

The government

With them

I think that they are in bed!

As "Apart from

An ethical issue,

We see nothing wrong

With it!"

They said!

Only three thousand Lions

Left in South Africa

In the wild to see!

With over eight thousand

Permanently caged

In 24/7 365 days

In captivity!

Without them ever going hunting

A buck to see!

Or even any possibility!

Of them ever being free!

As you can't release them

Into the wild unfortunately!

Now we have an enigma

Or will

Ultimately!

And why

Is all of this happening?

…….. For MONEY!!!

Music gives!

Music gives!

A soul to the Universe,

Wings to the mind!

Flight to the imagination!

And life to everything!

Add potent poetry

Then the heart and mind sing!

Nature's Symphony!

The fishing boats lights bobbing

One the evening sea!

As it floats on by

In peace and harmony!

The waves rumble in

Creating natural tranquility!

A healing thing for humanity!

Flamed wispy clouds above

Painting nature's celestial canopy!

What a glorious moment to be alive

At this seaside sanctuary!

No one around

Far as the eye can see!

Loving being in tune

With nature and her

Natural

Symphony!

No doubt!

"Do you know how many

People want me?"

"I do, without a doubt!"

I see them every time

That we go out!"

Oh Mother Earth!

Put yourself into space, just floating around,
With the stars and the peace to live by,
You look there in front, at this jewel in the sky,
What a wonderful sight for you and I.

Oh Mother Earth, the people down there,
Think that they are the important ones.
But if you study their behavior,
Their time down there is almost gone.

Oh Mother Earth, technology rules,
From computers to lasers and bombs,
Fighting and killing each other, never fair,
For what, does it matter, does anyone care?

Oh Mother Earth, the people down there,
Are never lost for verse,
But must be the craziest life form,
In the whole darn Universe.

Oh Mother Earth, we wish you well,
Can your nature withstand the pain?
Brought on by global warming,
Not to mention the acid rain.

Oh Mother Earth, they must be fools,
Because down there, Mother, money rules

With cities a rat race, run at a fast pace,
And the rich ones holding the jewels.

Oh Mother Earth, the problems down there,
Religions as varied as sight,
But all of the different worshippers,
Cannot possibly all be right?

Oh Mother Earth, their love it is thin,
As a lot hate each other,
For the pigment of their skin,
Live in peace, laugh with friends,
After all, we are only Homo sapiens.

Oh Mother Earth, the skies are burning,
Surely it's time the tide was turning,
From living fast, all push and shove,
The world must turn on to love.

Oh Mother Earth, we must clear this haze,
And start to untangle this global maze,
The scent of the flowers and a bird that sings,
Dear God lift the souls with eagle's wings.

Oh Mother Earth, the stresses and strains,
Millions of people are numbing their brains,
With numerous drugs, to lessen the pain,
The solution – the world must be born again.

Oh Mother Earth, will we win? Will we fail?
And one day Mother, will sanity prevail?
In future years, if you can see the sense,
Mankind could be past tense.

When you look from space,
With the stars and the peace to live by,
You shake your head,
And wonder to yourself,
Why?

Oh Mother Earth, GMOs in most of our food
Not natural, not doing our bodies any good!
Chemtrails spread from planes all over our skies
News and weather channels spreading disinformation and lies!

Oh Mother Earth, Geo-engineering, weather manipulation,
HAARP sending microwaves from many a base station,
Smart meters and 5G sending out their harmful waves invisibly
With many affected unknowingly!

Oh Mother Earth, the massive plastic pollution of the seas,
With Fukushima spreading Oceanic radiation and dis-ease,
Trophy hunters killing the best of each species to hang on their wall,
With high powered weapons and pride as the species in number fall!

Oh Mother Earth, extinction of species at an alarming rate,
With poaching syndicates helping to seal their fate,
In the last four hundred years while we watch cell phones, computers and TV,
We have managed to change our home in some cases irretrievably!

Oh Mother Earth, love and compassion are lacking,
With your crust and groundwater being broken and poisoned
By chemicals used in explosive fracking,
Many people are worried, living in fright,
When their tap water can be set alight,

Oh Mother Earth, is there any solution?
To the air, land and water pollution?

All the changes being made since the Industrial revolution,
Merely a blink of the eye in Universal time for all to see,
Are we fulfilling our God-given role of this planets protection and custody?

Oh Mother Earth, attacks happening without a soldiers foot on the ground!
As weaponised drones extinguish their chosen targets
Wherever they are to be found!
Controlled by people with a joystick in hand
Sitting in a far-off foreign land!

Oh Mother Earth, in space through the Cosmos we roam
Looking for planets with signs of water so we can find a new home,
Nuclear weapons abundant hidden in bunkers and submarines all over
With the capability of blowing this beautiful planet up over fifty times over,

Oh Mother Earth, What of God and Spirituality?
What is happening now is insanity!
In no way could it be described as funny
And all for a man-made creation,
For the love of power and money!

Oh Mother Earth, This compressed ball of stardust
That we all call home, wherever we were born or met,
Believe it or not is now in debt!

Crazy as it sounds, economically this is true,
It raises the question of in debt to who?

Oh Mother Earth, For all of our great creations, it makes an interesting tale,
With corporations running the planet, leaving many to wail.
Will common sense ever prevail?
Secret societies, bankers and other groups never to be taken for a fool,
Creating a New World Order to divide and rule!

Oh Mother Earth, Looking at the myriad stars in the blinking night sky
This is the only one where our Souls and Spirits can fly!
We must take care of our home a jewel in the sky to see,
If any aliens ever observed us they would think that we are crazy!

Oh Mother Earth, love does abound and in every mother
And lover is easily found; look in nature it is all around!
Music lifting hearts in symphony, setting Souls and Spirits free!
With its melody, rhythm and harmony, the symmetry of poetry!

Oh Mother Earth, Is this the future that you would like to see?
As we go spinning on into eternity!
One day mankind could easily be,

Written in history books as rulers of the planet for a short while,
But now they are History!

This poem was extended beyond the word "Why" after my return to Scotland

From South Africa after having lived there for over thirty six years.

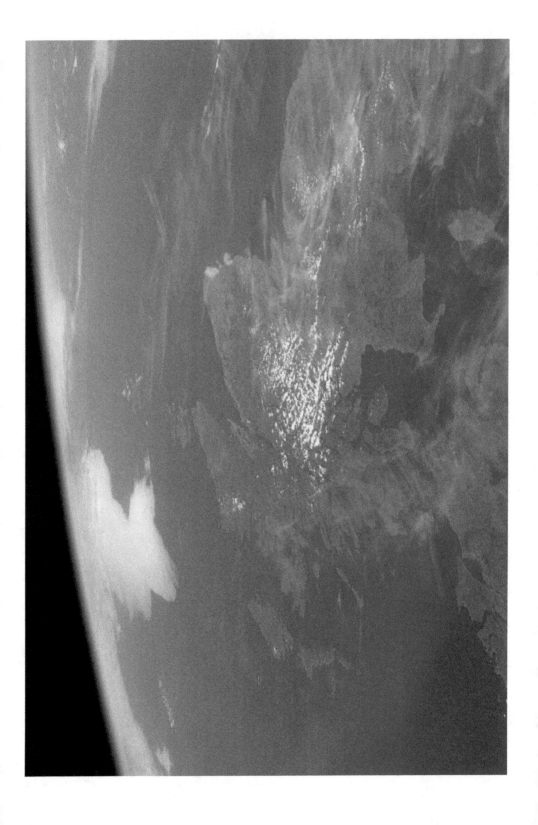

One way!

"Good morning!

I love you!"

What a way

To start a day!

When whispered in your ear,

In your mind it does stay!

No going astray!

This is truly love!

One way!

Pay out!

A friend was invited

To the Bravo lounge

At a private function

With some friends,

Music they were going to play!

Supposed to get paid,

They played for two hours,

Now two weeks later,

No sign of any pay!

"Sounds like a Casino to me!"

I said without a doubt!

"As they are renowned globally

For not wanting

To

Pay out!"

Poverty!

"Will you pay of my taxi debt?"

"I have amassed a bill of three thousand rand with him

Since we met!"

He used to also give me money

And would like to make me his honey!"

I also owe the other one six hundred and eighty rand!"

But please pay them both as

I don't have any money

Or income,

I am sure that you will understand!"

"I go to work each day

To earn an income so that my bills

I can pay!

Don't really have much extra

That is what I say, but I keep you alive,

Pay all your other bills,

From scans, prescriptions and doctors,

Booze, Fags, clothes and yet

You leave another man

As beneficiary

In your wills!"

Not to mention this fact

That not many see,

You have inherited the equivalent

Of the lottery!

But get angry

Whenever it is mentioned you see!

This does not go down well with me!

When you are pleading

Poverty!

Pussy!

I think we should

Start writing erotic poetry!

There would be a

Big market for that

I can see!

Writing about our own

Experiences!

Creating for others

A fantasy!

About erect

Pulsating penis!

And juicy

Pink

Pussy!

DAVID NICOLL AND FRIENDS

VOLUME 1

DAVID NICOLL

AND

FRIENDS

VOLUME 2

(REV 1)

DAVID NICOLL AND FRIENDS

VOLUME 3

Lawn!

A worker who was really pissed

Got his ex-boss back in a way

Not to be missed!

He had been laid off the previous week

And revenge he did seek!

He was not built big

Not heavy with brawn!

So he threw a mole

Over the fence,

Into his ex-bosses

Manicured lawn!

THE SEER

"You are not a poet,
You are in fact a bard,
And you are!!
What exactly did Helen mean?
A dictionary check
Would enlighten this scene.

A poet is one who likes to write in rhyme,
Or who has great imagination and creativity,
Most of the time.
A bard is
"One of an ancient order of Celtic Poets".
Also writers of rhyme but in built into your,
DNA and Heritage, most of the time.
A recollection to Washington,
At an international Poet's convention,
By a fellow Scots poet,
A man of wisdom and good cheer,
He referred to me not as,
David Nicoll,
But as "Macleod Of Macleod – "The Seer".

Training!

Down having a fag in the morning

Below my sons flat,

Is where I was at,

Then a neighbor

Comes down to throw his rubbish out,

He was surprised by the way I was dressed

Without a doubt!

The weather was changing

Had just started raining,

So I told him

"Excuse my dress,

I am a Buddhist monk

In training!

K9

The amazing thing
About some of
Nature's shapes
Is the lifelike
Look and feeling
That it partakes

Crouching on the hilltop
Looking mighty fine
Is the extremely alert
And smiling
K9

REMINISCING AGAIN

checking out the paragliding take off site,
too much wind, conditions not right,
memories coming back
from a previous day,
when Wayne, in the clouds
would play!

up in the air,
the soul and spirit
flying free,
until an ill wind
collapsed his chute,
no time to let out
the reserve,
just falling.........
constantly!

badly damaging his spine,
feeling the strain,
he is back
at the same spot
reminiscing again!

ONLY TOKING

Feet tapping good,
Soul food,
The Aquarian Quartet,
What a set!

Accoustic music
Taken to its extreme
Carried away
As if in a dream!

Highs and lows
As the rhythm flows,
World class
A harmonic cure,
To carry you away
For sure!

Legends in their own right,
In their own time,
Listen to the laid back
Symphonies,
Interact,
As if
In rhyme!

In the change room
With them, after the show,
Having a sociable chat,
Catching a blow,
Behind Steve's head
A sign says "No Smoking"
Just as well
That we were
Only toking!

ONCE

Never in my life
Have I been called
A ponce -
This photo with
Janine and Trissia
Has got to
Be called
"You only
Live
Once!"

INDEED

On the 5th of August 1962
An arrest was made
Of a man well known
To both me and you.

For twenty seven years
He languished in jail,
Coming out compassionate,
Forgiving,
Was it to any avail?

He went on to lead
The country from its apartheid days
To democracy,
One man, one vote
As the textbooks says.

A statesman to the world,
Such wisdom in his years,
Been through many ups and downs,
Much laughter and tears.

We salute you
Son of Africa,
Helping others in need.
Nelson Mandela
A very special person
Indeed!

LET IT PASS!

In the lush green meadow
By his grey mother's side
As she casts a wayward glance
At the fine young colt
Munching in her stride,
With the newborn's knobbly knees
And mouthful of grass
A moment in time
Has been captured to not
Let it pass!

Rainbow nation!

Massive media outrage at the American bow hunter

Who flew to Africa, travelling very far!

To come over and shoot with an arrow

Zimbabwe's biggest wildlife star!

Cecil the Lion

Was lured out of his Hwange wildlife sanctuary!

By unscrupulous hunters

Who wanted nothing other than

Something for their client to shoot

And of course, Money!

What people don't realize

Is that every day Lions on South Africa

Are shot in cages by this or another way!

By "Big Game hunters"

Who are rich and a large amount

They are willing to pay!

Bred for the bullet

Is the catchphrase today!

Eight thousand Lions in captivity

Treated like cattle, bred to die!

Just the same as cattle and sheep

Some people say!

But they are not eaten,

Just the skin and head taken!

The bones sent to China

For Tiger bone wine

And the meat, the muscle

Presumably

Thrown away!

What an indictment on mankind I say!

Hopefully this will bring about change

To highlight the situation

Of Canned Lion Hunting

In this the

Rainbow Nation!

Refuse!

"If all else fails

Hit them with Bullshit

They will never understand,

Then you can't lose!

Then make them an offer

That they

Cant

Refuse!"

Right!

"Is it going to be

Another power cut tonight?"

"Load shedding my ass!"

It always switches off

Just when you are settled down

And feeling right!"

Sale!

"This must have been what

Vernon was talking about!"

Kutala exclaimed

In a shout!

I didn't know what to do!

I was standing with my bowl of soup

In the ten o clock tea break

Microwave queue!

"Look at that!"

Marius said with some wit!

"It even has lumps of meat in it!"

"My God, are you guys for real?"

It can't be what he was talking about

As it is only a ONE course meal!

"We are only jealous!"

She did squeal!

"Tell us where you buy it!

I would love to buy

One for a meal!"

So now to bring

And end to this tale!

I am thinking of offering

"Shakeenahs soup!"

In the drawing office

For sale!

Second hand store!

Saw a one armed man

In a second hand store

And told him

"Sir, I don't think

That you will find

What you are

Looking for!"

Shit!

Sometimes my lady is funny,

Full of wit!

But sometimes,

She has

Mental constipation

And is full

Of

Shit!

THE SEER

"You are not a poet,
You are in fact a bard,
And you are!"
What exactly did Helen mean?
A dictionary check
Would enlighten this scene.
A poet is one who likes to write in rhyme.
Or who has great imagination and creativity,
Most of the time.
A bard is
"One of an ancient order of Celtic Poets".
Also writers of rhyme but in built into your,
DNA and Heritage, most of the time.
A recollection to Washington,
At an international Poet's convention,
By a fellow Scots poet,
A man of wisdom and good cheer.
He referred to me not as,
David Nicoll,
But as "Macleod Of Macleod - "The Seer".

SUN!

Rainbows
In the rainbow nation
Ending on
Standing stones.

Moments in time
Moments of
Fleeting light,
Double rainbows
Cutting the
Sky from dark
To light!

A change in
Weather
The rain
Has gone
From
African
Rain
To
African
Sun!

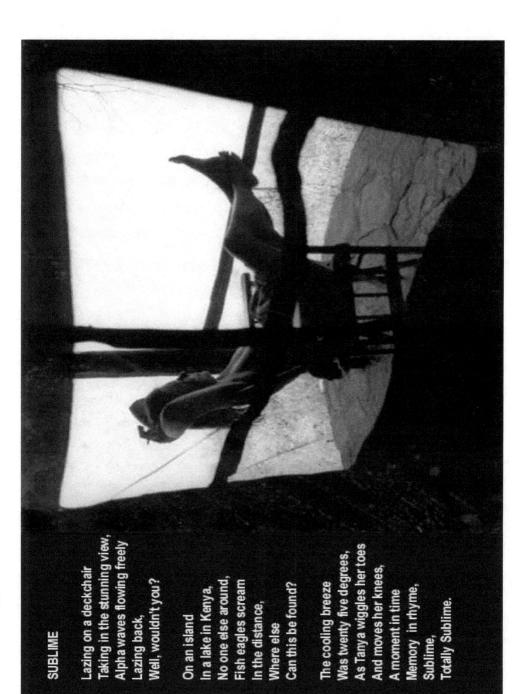

SUBLIME

Lazing on a deckchair
Taking in the stunning view,
Alpha waves flowing freely
Lazing back,
Well, wouldn't you?

On an island
In a lake in Kenya,
No one else around,
Fish eagles scream
In the distance,
Where else
Can this be found?

The cooling breeze
Was twenty five degrees,
As Tanya wiggles her toes
And moves her knees,
A moment in time
Memory in rhyme,
Sublime,
Totally Sublime.

The Dark!

High above the valley
Early morning mist
Beyond the trees
Starts to rise.

Looking over KwaZulu Natal
Valley of 1000 Hills,
A natural silence,
For a moment,
Then the sounds
Start to come alive.

Cockerels start to crow,
Dogs start to bark,
As the sun slowly
Brightens the world
To daylight
From dark!

SCOTS!

Having met Marti Pellow
Of Wet, Wet, Wet,
And Paul, the lead singer
Of Sugardrive,
Some similarities
We have met.

Like how do they do it?
Was it in their genes?
Or is it like drawing lots?
The response from both people
Was because,
We are Scots!

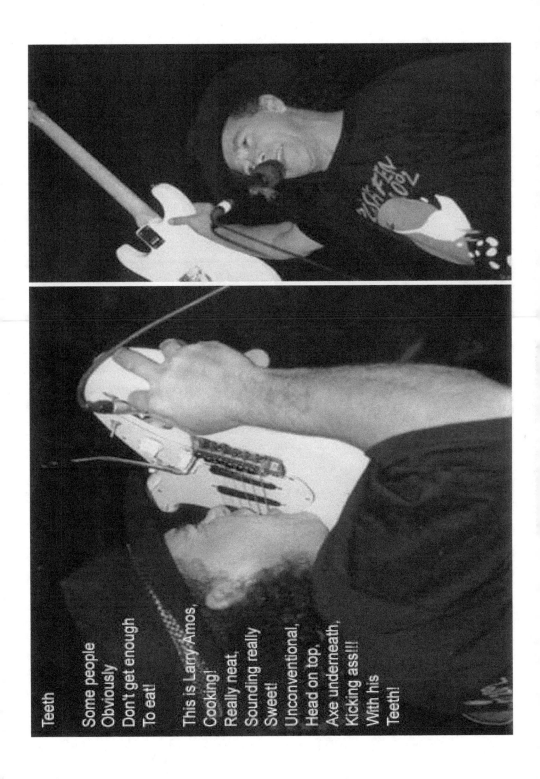

Teeth

Some people
Obviously
Don't get enough
To eat!

This is Larry Amos,
Cooking!
Really neat,
Sounding really
Sweet!
Unconventional,
Head on top,
Axe underneath,
Kicking ass!!!
With his
Teeth!

SEEING!

Fruits of the summer,
Fruits of the season,
Each a natural
Work of art,
Supplied by our creator,
For food, sustenance
Colour and well being,
The pleasure of tasting and
Seeing!

Scotsmen! (Dramatic!)

Scotsmen!

Yeah, they can be jovial

While following a team!

With the kilt on

They can be a local

Lasses dream!

Leaving some moments

Not to be missed!

After getting

Extremely inebriated!

Otherwise known

As pissed!

They can make you ecstatic!

Or make you sick!

Never to be classified

As boring!

But

Rather

Dramatic!

Written after Dr Joubert mentioned how

Scotsmen can be dramatic!

Seeing You!

Doctor

I need to update you on the question that you did ask!

Otherwise some inaccurate answers by me

And you could put me to task!

I said that she was only drinking milk stout!

But that is not now true!

As she has had quite a few

Concoctions

Since seeing you!

Shapes!

"Twenty Courtleigh please!"

"Do you want a cellphone or a laptop?"

Asked the jovial lady attendant!

"Have a won a prize?"

I did loudly chant!

Bubbly lady!

Make no mistakes!

"It is so that

I know what you want

As the boxes

Are

Different shapes!

Sheep!

Think of happy sheep

When going to sleep!

To put a smile on your face!

It will get you to sleep!

With a moment to keep!

Positive mental thoughts

Of happy sheep!

Situation!

What a situation

What a scene!

Racism is alive and well

In South Africa today!

With hatred and poisoned souls

Taking up the day!

With this curse

Ever go away?

Why is this?

Will we ever win?

And realize that

The only difference between

Us Homo Sapiens

Is the colour of our skin!

Under the skin,

We are all the same!

Globally that is

Not just here!

Go to other parts of Africa

You will find no racism in some places

Only kind words

And smiles on faces!

Here,

You are classified

Dependent on your skin colour

And what your

Race is!

This really is an

Ongoing situation

In what was once

In the days of Nelson Mandela

Known as the

Rainbow nation!

What a

Situation!

So far away!

So far away!

So far away!

I wish that together

We could stay!

Love flies over the Ocean

From me to you!

And also the other way too!

Missing you madly

Would love to hug you gladly!

So far away!

So far away!

I wish that together

We could stay!

Imagine now that I am holding you tight!

We are together as one this very night!

As I squeeze you tight!

As I squeeze you tight!

So far away!

So far away!

I wish that together

We could stay!

Something back!

Keith had been working

For a long time

On Lulu's fathers flat!

No mention of price

For labour!

Keith didn't mention that!

"So how much do I owe you?"

Lulu's father was heard to say!

Then Keith replied

That "It was OK!

As he didn't have to pay!"

"Why not?"

He did sing!

"Because we are getting married

Next year and

You are paying

For the wedding!"

"Look at it as a form of Lobola!"

Keith said in good crack!

Which is really great

And a way

If giving something back!

Spare?

This morning I had a situation

That was well worth it to see!

Almost like something from

A Leon Schuster movie!

The car wouldn't start!

Battery totally flat!

So I asked Elmar

If he could help me

With jump leads!

He lives in the upstairs flat!

So down he comes

And away we go!

Connect up the jump leads,

Then charge it quickly

Not slow!

After a couple of minutes

The Mercedes engines

Spark plugs

Fire up!

So ecstatic now

And ready to go!

Out now to disconnect the cable!

And planning to go to the

Battery Centre in Mossel bay

While I am able!

Then something happens

Which is really not fun!

While I am outside

The cars central locking

Switches on!

Oh my goodness me!

How are we going to

Sort out this

Potential calamity?

The doors won't open

Passenger side window

Slightly down as we

Stand momentarily

Each with a frown!

We tray a wire

Bent into a hook

And a big wooden spoon,

Engine ticking over merrily

Me thinking it's going to

Run out of petrol soon!

Eventually we get to the

Door latch and find

That it will not open!

Central locking only

Get's overridden on the

Drivers side!

Not exactly what I

Was hopin!

"We will have to try the

Drivers door!"

Says he to me!

As some long wire started

To get twisted by Elmar and Shelly!

I wonder if this will work?

I thought hesitantly!

So over the space

The twisted wire snakes!

Slowly, slowly through

The steering wheel,

Edging closer,

Ever closer!

Real tension

No mistakes!

Onto the door catch

The improvised opener loops!

As he pulled it back

It slipped off!

Just as we were about to

Let out whoops!

So I held on the outside

The handle for the door!

As the same actions

Were repeated once more!

After three tries,

There were shouts

To the skies

As the door

Became ajar!

"Wonderful!

Wonderful!

Thank you!

You are a star!"

He also gave me

Some good advice

For free!

It came with no price!

Standing now

My fingers running through my hair!

He said

"Your car keys!

Maybe you should get

A spare?"

She's got Soul!

Chorus:

She's got Soul!

She's got Soul!

Her mind and body are beyond control!

She's got Soul!

She's got Soul!

Dancing with the music

Flowing with the breeze!

Floating in nature

With the greatest of ease!

She's got Soul!

She's got Soul!

Her mind and body are beyond control!

She's got Soul!

She's got Soul!

Cooking in the kitchen

Cooking in the bed!

This lady has got Soul like I said!

Singing and playing

Listen to the poetry she is saying,

Blessing and praying!

She's got Soul!

She's got Soul!

Her mind and body are beyond control!

She's got Soul! She's got Soul!

Sound!

Wake to a beautiful morning

With peace all around!

Shakeenah and myself

At peace listening

To natures sound!

Still there!

Memories, memories of bygone days!

Where as a youth I was full of life, exuberant,

Long hair, a hippie in training,

Walking around windswept

Scottish island bays!

A romance with an older lady!

A turn on for us both is what I say!

Sparked by loosening our inhibitions

With a bottle of Mateus rose!

Red flushed cheek, knees feeling weak!

Both of us entranced with the need for satisfaction

That we did seek!

Moments in time, totally sublime!

As the day turned to night

Nothing else mattered

It felt so right!

Now many years have passed,

Since then some losing, some winning!

Both of us now closer to the end of our lives

Than the beginning!

A unique situation beyond compare!

The memories, love and passion

Are still there!

Sunshine!

So here's to the weekend!

Friday morning and all is fine

The boss has today off

So we all at work will shine!

And tonight

Let's braai some meat!

Drink some beer and wine!

So glad in my heart

That my beautiful lady

Is mine!

Bring on

The sunshine!

Symphony!

You are truly blessed David!

To be in love with

Such s beautiful multi-talented lady!

Who loves you deeply too!

Making music with guitar and djembe drums!

We love to play and sing!

One of our soon to be global inventions

Is Bum Drumming!

Loving and at times in tune with nature,

With the waves crashing their melody!

As we create with Shakeenah

Building standing and balancing stone sculptures

For others to see!

And me, of it and her

Taking amazing photography!

I would like to say"Thank you!"

To the Universe and God

For bringing you together with me

In our

Symbiotic symphony!

The big man!

Just got a message from my Daughter Lisa

Last night!

"Sorry to tell you this

But your cousin Rodney passed away!

Everything before that was alright!

I don't know what to say!

They just found him that way!"

It came as a shock

As he was always as

Solid as a rock!

I am lost for words

Don't know what to say!

Other than I am sorry!

He lived in Stornoway!

Life is so short!

We are here

But for a moment in time!

Sometimes tough!

Sometimes sublime!

You never know

When it is your turn

To go!

Enjoy life when you can!

Regardless of circumstance!

There is no guarantee

That you will get

Another chance!

Hope that you

Leave something behind

And no doubt will still be in

Many a mind!

When a loved one passes away

It makes you think twice

About the impermanence of your stay!

This is very true!

It can also act as a catalyst

For what you still have to do!

It can bring focus

To getting into reality

What is still in your mind!

Whether a painting, sculpture,

Poetry, songs or voice recordings

For the blind!

Live life to the full

For as long as you can!

As one day

You will be away on that

Astral flight to meet up with

The Big Man!

That As well!

"I am going to drink myself

Single tonight!"

Is the story Myra

Did tell!

I thought

"Some men

Do that

As well!"

12/09/2018 21:21

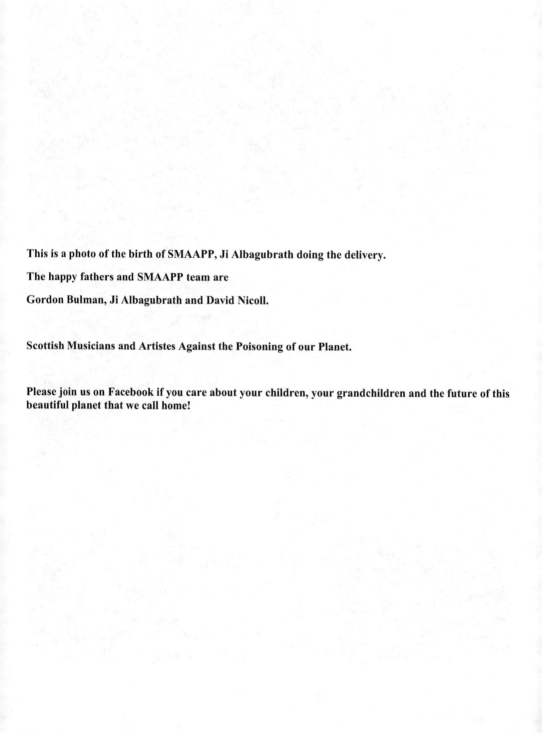

This is a photo of the birth of SMAAPP, Ji Albagubrath doing the delivery.

The happy fathers and SMAAPP team are

Gordon Bulman, Ji Albagubrath and David Nicoll.

Scottish Musicians and Artistes Against the Poisoning of our Planet.

Please join us on Facebook if you care about your children, your grandchildren and the future of this beautiful planet that we call home!

The flow!

Complexities in nature!

Loving weekends to the full!

Then comes Monday!

Back to work!

And sometimes

Mentally not so cool!

Taking your frustrations

Out on others

Like a fool!

Losing pace

In the rat race!

Although the rat

Down here goes slow!

Forgetting my motto!

"Hakuna Matata!

And going

With

The

Flow!

The MAD story!

"Here, listen to this!" Mervyn Fuller said," I have written a song from one

Of the poems in your book Thoughts and Reflections!

I had given him a copy of it a month before!

So was born the band MAD (Mervyn And Dave!)

It progressed from there to Mervyn phoning me from time to time and giving

Me a prompt to write the lyrics for a song from!

I was working in Lephalale, Limpopo province and Mervyn lives in Gordon's bay,

Western Cape!

An example of what would happen is this! He phoned me once on a Saturday

Morning at ten thirty! "You should write something about Friends!"

I was visiting a friend at the time, got a writing pad and sat down at his

Dining room table and wrote the lyrics for what is now the song of the same name!

Our first song was created in January 2012! Since then,

We have released two CDs called Treat it so! And This is MAD2!

Our next CD titled On days like these! is due to be released in February 2015.

After writing the lyrics/poetry, I would type it out and email it to Mervyn,

He would then come up with a structure, rhythm and style for our new baby!

Will it be rock, reggae, soul etc?

He would then lay down the tracks putting guitar, drums etc and pull in

Assistance from his friends Mike Laatz on saxophone and Mike Pregnolatu

On lead guitar and keyboards!

We are both Spiritual men although not religious, the content of many

Of our songs are thought provoking and healing in one form or another

To be heard by generations to come and help in its own way!

What started as a thought,

The plant has now grown tall!

For a band called MAD!

Who it turns out,

Are not so MAD

After all!

THE BEST
OF
MAD

MERVYN FULLER

DAVID NICOLL

TREAT IT SO !

A POETIC AND MUSICAL COLLABORATION
BY
MERVYN FULLER
AND
DAVID NICOLL

Mervyn fuller
And
David nicoll

THIS IS M A D 2 !
A POETIC AND MUSICAL COLLABORATION

Mervyn And David
FULLER   NICOLL
A MUSICAL AND POETIC COLLABORATION

Wolves are the most amazing caring and intelligent animals. I once had a pack of six, started with a White Artic Wolf female and then got a black Canadian Timber Wolf and they bred. Kept some of the amazingly coloured hybrids.

All was well for many years but it became a problem when the full moon was shining and their hunting instinct kicked in. It did not matter what reinforcements that I added to the boundary fence they would find a way through, going under through or over it.

This created great stress for many in the local community in Assegay, KwaZuluNatal in South Africa as there was a conservancy next to me and they would go hunting buck as a pack in the neighbouring conservancy.

When the female is pregnant she digs a curved tunnel into the hillside normally with the entrance being under a bush for concealment. The tunnel curves round on the inside into a chamber at the end. She then goes in and pushes up the loose earth in front of her so that all that is visible is a slit along the top of the earth wall. She has the pups in there and stays inside for three to four days without eating or drinking. After about four weeks the pups emerge from the tunnel to greet the world. At this stage they look like small bears. Bundles of hair and barrel shaped. They are so beautiful, inquisitive and playful with each other. When they are big enough to leave the den the mother nudges them off the rough platform at the tunnel entrance and they slide down the rocky scree. She then picks them up at the bottom by the back of the neck and takes them to a new safe above ground location. She is extremely protective towards them. The amazing thing about Wolves howling is that they all start at exactly the same moment then howl for a couple of minutes and then all stop at the same moment as well. This can be at any time. I do not know why they do this. At the end I was forced to get rid of them due to their instinctive hunting habits and had to find a new home for them.

The SPCA did not have space and would have put them down. This was not an option. I was thinking that maybe a farmer would love to have them for safety and security and I wanted them to stay together. Ended up contacting Sally Scott who had written a previous article about me and them for The Crest magazine in Hillcrest.

She did a write up explaining the situation and it was published in the press. I was then contacted by Larry Paul from The HuskyRomi Wolf Sanctuary in Reitz, Free State.

He told me that he would take them all to his Wolf Sanctuary. After that I was contacted by a lady from the TV programme 50/50 who said that she had been informed of my situation and would like to come down and film it.

So that next weekend they both arrived at the same time and Larry and myself proceeded to put them with some difficulty into the cages on his trailer. All the while that this was happening we were being filmed.

The younger Wolves were skittish and running away from us so he decided to tranquilise them using his rifle and tranquilizer darts.

This was traumatizing to watch and Cindy my Zulu lady at that time was freaked out thinking that they were being shot. After some time they were all loaded and the trailer departed from my driveway. A sudden silence enveloped the place; it was so quiet with no life around.

This was without a doubt one of the worst days of my life to have my Wolf family taken from me.

Solitude, silence and loneliness came over me and then depression. I lost all interest in developing my home any further and used to stay away for extended periods before ultimately selling the place.

I have visited the HuskyRomi Wolf Sanctuary a couple of times to see them. Larry looks after at that time over 170 of the most magnificent Wolves that I have ever seen. He does this on a voluntary basis and relies on donations from the public to do so as well as paid guided tours of the Wolves pens. Please look at his Facebook page and you will see these magnificent creatures or visit him if you are going that way.

On arriving there on my first visit I was waiting at the office some distance away when they all started howling in unison.

Never in my life have I heard such a thing. Thank you Larry Paul for what you did for me and for still to this day looking after them.

He takes in Wolves from all over South Africa as they all have the same traits and ultimately need to be rescued.

If you are so inclined any donations to his Wolf Sanctuary would be greatly appreciated by him and the Wolves survival is dependent on these.

They did show a very informative programme on 50/50 about the introduction of Wolves to South Africa. My only comment would be that I do not agree with her comment at the very end of the programme.

I miss my Wolves.

The Wolves!

Trophy hunters!

Taking out the best genes!

Taking out the best seed!

Diminishing the prime

Gene pool!

In the name of conservation!

The Wolves

Are in the

Hen house

Indeed!

The Score!

Went for an ECG today!

Never been for one before

But I was feeling OK!

Got all strapped up with the sensors

To my chest, all OK,

She said "Just

Lie down and rest!"

Then onto the treadmill

Also a first time,

Your feet can't stand still!

So off we go!

The machine going slow!

Then it gets quicker!

My feet can't stand still, have to

Keep on walking!

As the sister to me kept talking!

"Are you OK?

Do you want to rest!

"No problem sister!

I am feeling alright!

Then a thought as I burst into song!

Creating smiles

"Well I would walk

Five hundred miles

And I would walk five hundred more!"

That brightened her day!

You know the score!

There!

Japie, "The Newspaper!"
Used to always stand in front of
Mossel bay's fisherman's square!
The reason that he was called that

Is because he was very observant

And could tell you

What was happening with whom?

Why and where?

He was there in all weathers

With his grey grizzled beard!

Spent a lifetime at sea,

From no other's

Was he feared!

Then one day

He was there no more!

"Where has the newspaper gone?"

Everyone wanted to know!

What is the score?

He was always talking about leaving!

Someone was going to offer him a job!

He was an honest peaceful man,

Never one to rob!

Then news came back

Which left everyone with a frown!

Japie had moved to Boksburg

Was cycling on a bike

When a taxi ran him down!

Sometimes life is sad!

It is not always fair!

You are sorely missed Japie!

When we look at the corner,

We miss

The Newspaper

There!

This Time!

Been without my car for six long weeks!

Stuck in Mossel bay, not exactly getting the pleasures

That I seeks!

Got it back just yesterday,

Now it won't start this morning!

Exactly the same, "Injector problem!"

Sun shining but still stuck

What a day!

Met some interesting people

Although depressed,

Not really sweet!

As every weekend

I would travel this town

On my feet!

Waiting on Johann the mechanic coming

"I will be there now!"

He did say!

That was two hours ago

And all he can really do

Is once more

Take my car away!

A Renault Megane 1.9 Dci

When it is running

With the roof off,

A pleasure in life

At one with the sky!

So I sit and wait,

Pondering my fate!

As the clock does slowly chime

And wondering

"How long will I

Be without it

This time?"

Thrown out!

Been staying with my lady, my lover!

She is great with the housework

But has a habit of sticking stuff undercover!

Piles will appear on surface or on floor!

Under blanket, towel or dishcloth

When she doesn't want to look at what

Is under it anymore!

All sweet, looks neat!

She loves music playing guitar

And getting into the djembe drum grooves

Then every now and again

And undercover piles

Mysteriously moves!

I lifted one big cover just yesterday

And was flabbergasted I must say!

There were the missing big cast iron pots!

Filled with rotting vegetables, water

And soaken newspaper, like lots!

The oven tray was also there

Beyond compare

Like a massive petri dish!

With sporing mould

Sprouting around the rotting food!

This is a real health hazard!

Not at all good!

We both hold lots

Of dreams and wishes,

The problem is that she

Just hates doing the dishes!

So like a dumb waiter!

The dirty pots pans and tupperware

Get put under cover for later!

But later never comes

As we miss the pans and pots

Next time I will know

Where they are,

No need to draw lots!

What is this?

I originally did think

With a metre high covered

Pile of stuff next

To the sink!

That makes me think!

And no doubt drink!

So now the Tupperware

Has hit the rubbish bag!

Still filled with the contents

What a drag!

The pots are still waiting attention!

To scrub them is my intention!

There is really very little else

That I can do as they are almost brand new!

The cast iron pans need boiling and oiling

To get rid of the rust!

In God we both trust!

All will be right

Without a doubt

With new intentions now

When we are finished eating

Anything left over

Must either hit a compost bin

Or be thrown out!

To Cliffy!

"So great each other

Once again to see!

By total

Serendipity!

Fly!

Lift my Spirits father

Make them high!

I am in Knysna again

And want

To fly!!!

Too!

The lady with all the psychological sisters

Is fun that is true!

So beautiful and intelligent!

But you sometimes don't know!

Who you are talking too!

Thursday!

A daughter asked her mother a question

Which for her to answer was hard!

"Mommy, when can I give my Dad

His father's day card?"

She really didn't know

What to say but said

"Give it to him

When he delivers

The milk

On Thursday!"

To History

Shelter for
The Lewis families
From centuries ago,
Insulated from the
Westerly gales
And winter's snow

Using local resources
Earth filled rock
For the wall,
Covered by thatch
Animals living in
One end,
People in the other
On each side of an entrance hall!

Bonnochs (Scottish bread)
Cooked on the griddle
On the ever burning,
Peat fire
Wisping scented
Smoke
In the middle!

In balance with nature
Sleeping on mattresses
Made from straw,
No midgies* would enter
As everyone saw

Unfortunately
No more to be,
As the black houses
Have been relegated
To history

*one of the most irritating wee black stinging insects found on the planet

Photograph taken at the Arnol Black House Museum, The Isle of Lewis, Western Isles Scotland

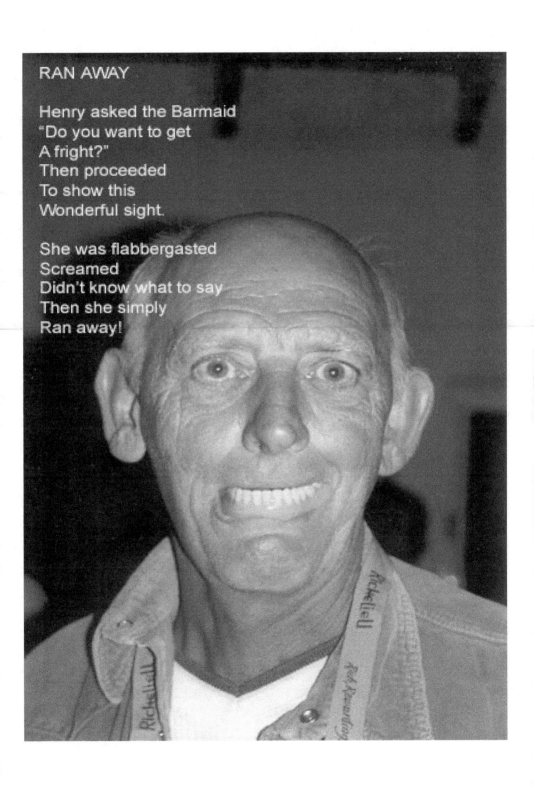

RAN AWAY

Henry asked the Barmaid
"Do you want to get
A fright?"
Then proceeded
To show this
Wonderful sight.

She was flabbergasted
Screamed
Didn't know what to say
Then she simply
Ran away!

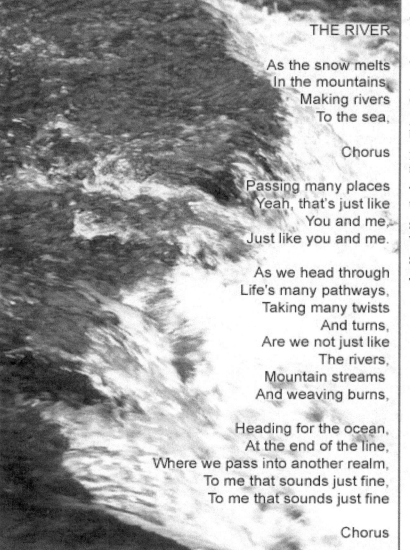

THE RIVER

As the snow melts
In the mountains,
Making rivers
To the sea,

Chorus

Passing many places
Yeah, that's just like
You and me,
Just like you and me.

As we head through
Life's many pathways,
Taking many twists
And turns,
Are we not just like
The rivers,
Mountain streams
And weaving burns,

Heading for the ocean,
At the end of the line,
Where we pass into another realm,
To me that sounds just fine,
To me that sounds just fine

Chorus

To sit!

This is said

A bit tongue in
cheek

And using a
bit of wit!

But my penis
is so polite

That it stands
up

So that girls
will have

Somewhere

To sit!

ZOOM

Like a bright yellow flower
Bursting in full bloom
The snow white cockatoo
Has just decided
To make his hair
Zoom!

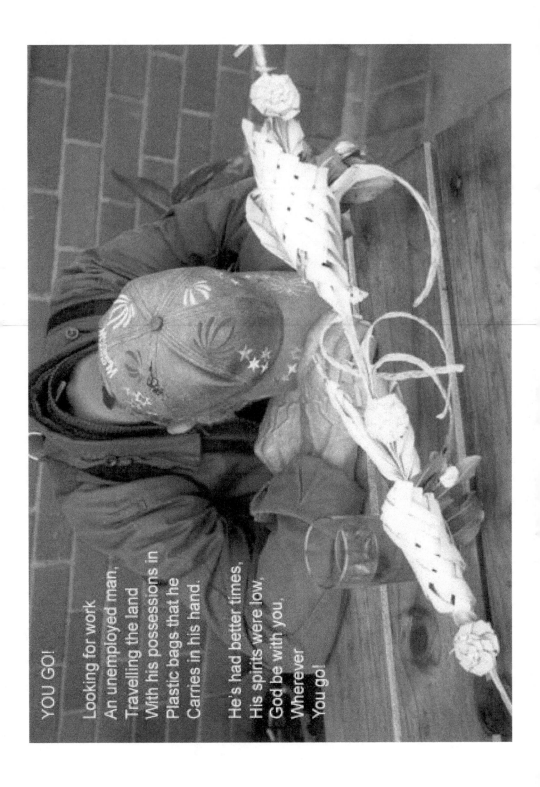

YOU GO!

Looking for work
An unemployed man,
Travelling the land
With his possessions in
Plastic bags that he
Carries in his hand.

He's had better times,
His spirits were low,
God be with you,
Wherever
You go!

MIGHT NOT BE SO CLEAR

A little experiment which
Will open your eyes,
And possibly even elicit
Some sights,
Concentrate on the the white
Dot on the nose
For 30 seconds, don't deviate
Forget the prose.
Then switch your view below,
Concentrate on the black dot
An image will appear,
Have no fear
Your own interpretation
"Might not be so clear".

.

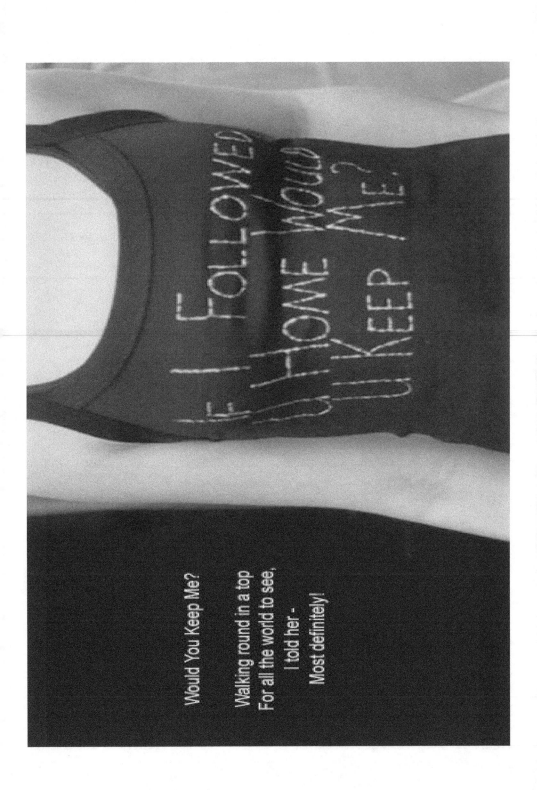

Would You Keep Me?

Walking round in a top
For all the world to see,
I told her -
Most definitely!

TRANQUILLITY!

An experience of a lifetime,
that's what I would say,
we saw about one hundred and thirty
dolphins in the bay today.

Some babies swimming
next to their mothers
sheltering alongside,
as they moved synchronistically
with the swell and the tide.

Beaks popping up,
fins appearing
in an effortless flow,
then down once more,
they slip below,
and into the water we go!

There was squeaking and clicking
as they passed
in the warm pristine sea
moving slowly by,
in peace and
tranquility!

TO THE GREAT WHITE HUNTERS

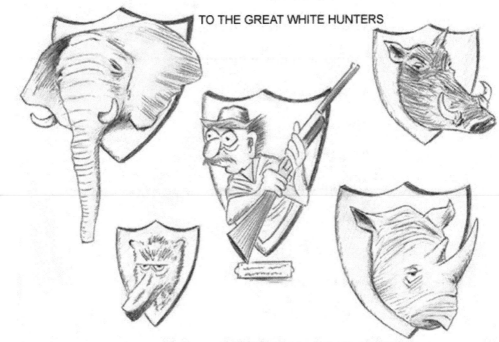

To the great white hunters, who now number few,
This is a story, especially for you,
Your trophies hang, on all of your walls,
And armed with your guns, you've got lots of balls.
In your own mind, what you do is right,
And you can kill any animals, in your sight,
You pay your dollars, making the farmers rich,
Shooting the biggest and the best, oh! what a bitch.
Your gallery is a reminder, of what one man can do,
And for the animal kingdom, a still-life, stuffed zoo,
When your days are over, your body we'll dry freeze,
And hang on your wall, next to the other trophies,
With a caption, "Great White Hunter" - he killed all of these!

View!

Met a beautiful young lady

Who is sure to go far!

She told me that

When asked as a teenager

"What would you like to be

When you grow up?"

She replied

"A porn star!"

Having travelled around

In many a nation!

Mentioned to her

One morning

"Now it is time

For congratulation!"

"Why is that?

What did you do?"

"Well, I have just made

Your dream

Come true!

Anonymously!!!

With a close

Up view!

Wave!

Is this someone in Eskom

With a sick sense of humour?

We were load shed for six till eight thirty,

Came on again for two minutes!

Then off again!

Think that I am getting a

Stress tumour!

Precious moments under candlelight!

In the year 2015, something's not right!

Moments to remember, moments to save!

Memories of when our ancestors

Lived in a cave!

If it comes on again,

The food will go

Immediately into

The Microwave!

Weekend!

My lady!

My lady!

My lover!

My friend!

I can feel it

In my heart

That we are

Going to have

A

Wonderful

Weekend!

I love you!

Where I am!

"What would be your ideal job?

Something that you would really enjoy

And have fun?"

Had to think about that one,

The question being asked by an agent

In London, in winter,

Well away from the sun!

"It should be at the coast!!

Next to the blue sea!

I should also live with a

Beautiful lady!

It should be long term!

Going on for years!

Be near to places like

Knysna and Cape Town!

Where we could make music

With great friends

Much laughter and very

Few tears!

I should like to work

Only eight hours per day

As the ten and twelve hour shifts

Lead my mind astray!

"Do you have any positions like that?"

To him I did ask,

"Hmmmm, no, not quite!"

His brain now being

Put to task!

Nowadays our emails are full of spam

So I told him

"Well, in that case

I think that I will just

Stay in Mossel bay

Where I am!"

Wife!

I never ever

Would have said in my life!

That I would end up

With a

Pastors

Wife!

Wishes!

Lots want my lady

When she is tidily dressed!

Am I cursed?

Or am I blessed?

Due to actions

And reactions

It sometimes leaves me

Distressed

And depressed!

But Hakuna Matata

Live for the moment

We are together

Sharing cuddles

And kisses!

You, all of you

On the other hand

Are merely

Expressing

Wishes!

Words!

From Talia Le Grance

Painting is poetry

That is seen

Rather than felt

And poetry is painting

That is felt

Rather than seen!

Leonardo Da Vinci

Painting pictures of mountains

Rivers or birds

Is also possible in poetry

Using only

Words!

Wouldn't you?

She has sex appeal

In percent about

One hundred and fifty two!

Men's head's turn

When she passes

And some women too!

There is little that

They can do!

All with one thing in mind!

Her I would like to screw!

Wouldn't you?

Xenophobia!

No need for Xenophobia!

In this day and age!

We are all the same!

Regardless of your

Life's stage!

Don't hold rage!

It is totally insanity

To see!

An innocent human being!

A Homo Sapien!

The same as you and me!

Being hacked down

So cruelly!

And mercilessly!

This is not our future!

It shall not be!

Our future is

In Nelson Mandela's dreams!

So mote it be!

Yogi tea poetic symphony!

The following sayings have been taken
From the labels on Yogi tea bags!
With poetry added to them.

Never try to impress others,
Try to impress yourself!
Do it, go for it!
Don't sit on the shelf!

Say it straight,
Simple and with a smile!
This will see you doing it
In style!

Empty yourself
And let the Universe fill you!
Is this not the best
Thing to do?

By honoring your words
You are honored too!
Let your heart
Guide you!

Life is a gift,

Truth is everlasting!
Whether you are
Eating or fasting!

Where is common sense?
Our intuition comes
From innocence!

Mental happiness
Is total relaxation!
Wherever you are
And in every nation!

Be proud of who you are,
Let your heart guide you!
To your friends and family
Forever stay true!

Compassion has no limit!
Kindness has no enemy!
Honesty will
Set yourself free!

An attitude of gratitude
Brings opportunities!
Giving thanks
Releases dis-ease!

Love is a source of

Bliss and infinity!

As in lovers eyes

Everyone can see!

Life is a flow of love

Your participation is requested!

As relief from being

Mentally pressured and tested!

Walk beautifully,

Talk beautifully,

Live beautifully,

Then your life you will see,

Can be lived beautifully!

Live through consciousness,

Not through emotion!

Keep your heart, head and spirit

In motion!

Trust is the union

Of intelligence and integrity!

Love is ecstasy!

Set yourself free!

Set yourself free!

Your Destiny!

Are we all just

Pawns in the game

Of global power

And mastery?

Where situations

Dependant on your

Actions and words

Are creating pain

Or harmony?

Due to circumstances

And present situations

Are you free?

Or is someone

Trying to

Deviate

Your

Destiny?

My friend Tomislav Svorinic and myself collaborated on some poem/photo combinations, RIP Tomi, here they are:

Again!

For the people of Knysna!

It brings out the best in humanity
After a natural calamity!

Over four hundred and thirty homes
Gone in an instant in time!
Everything gone,
Some left with just a pile of ash!
Not at all sublime!

Knysna! Jewel of the garden route!
Its warm people and ambiance
Which for many, many visitors
Is an ideal suit!

So many families
As we all know!
Were victims of
A raging inferno!

Step by step
And day by day!
Picking up the pieces
Of their lives,
There is no other way!

Bringing the community together
Strengthening the bond!
Studying the ashes!
Memories flashing!
Of which you are fond!

Many, many people love you!
This is true!
And in your hour of need!
Supplies, volunteers
And messages of condolences
Are flying through!

May your Souls rest in peace!
To the ones
Who did not make it through!

Copyright   David Nicoll   12.06.2017

Behind!

Loves depth is only known
When it is gone!
A statement by another,
Which is definitely true!
As many can attest to!

Mother's, father's
Sons, daughters,
Brothers, sisters,
Husbands, wives and lovers!
Missing relatives and friends now
Some lying alone, lonely
Under the covers!

Life is a gift!
Only temporary!
As we all have a limited time
This planet and its people to interact with,
Appreciate and see!

Make the most of each moment
In the present time!
And let your love flow!
As you never know!
Who's turn next
That it is to go?

A point to bear in mind!
Is that love is also
What you leave
Behind!

State Capture Gives Me The Blues

Talk of State Capture
In the government!
Billions of Rands
Stolen or misspent!
Talk of State Capture
In the government!

Minister of Finance!
You want the job?
Do what we tell you
Then we can rob!
Talk of State Capture
In the government!

Law unto themselves
Do what they will!
Bribery and corruption
Will make us ill!
Talk of State Capture
In the government!

Thuli's report when will we see?
Sure to create disharmony!
Talk of State Capture
In the government!

Media covers do we see
With own newspaper and TV!
Talk of State Capture
In the government!

I Wish!

I wish you beauty
The flowers in the spring
I wish you music from the sweet birds that sing
I wish you peace by the gentle stream
And guidance by the Spirit in the ultimate scheme
I wish you health
I wish you wealth
I wish you gold in store
I wish you heaven right here on earth and after death
Now what can I wish you more?

photo by Tomislav ©2013   words by David Nicol ©2011

The following pages are random shots and precious memories from my past:

The
KNYSNA
Poets

15/09/2016

Steve Newman

Sometimes things don't work out

The way that you planned,

That much I know

So here is an award

In a squint photo!

CPSIA information can be obtained
at www.ICGtesting.com
Printed in the USA
LVHW081254050219
606462LV00017B/256/P

9 781730 844577